To Mary

with my friendliest

[signature]

De Mr. 29. 0A.

EIGHT YEARS AS PRIME MINISTER
A PERSONAL VISION OF SPAIN 1996-2004

 Planeta

JOSÉ MARÍA
AZNAR

EIGHT YEARS AS PRIME MINISTER

A PERSONAL VISION OF SPAIN 1996-2004

 Planeta

© José María Aznar, 2004
© Editorial Planeta, S.A.
    Diagonal, 662-664, 08034 Barcelona (Spain)

Translated © Lisa Dillman, 2005

Original title: José María Aznar. Ocho años de gobierno

First edition in Spanish: May 2004
First edition in English: April 2005
Second edition in English: June 2005

ISBN: 0-9748724-7-4
Planeta Publishing Corp.
2057 N.W. 87 av.
Miami, Fl 33172 (USA)

Printed in Printer Colombiana S. A.

Table of Contents

For Ana, my wife,
and José María, Ana, and Alonso.
Without them, nothing would be possible.

Preface

This is not a memoir, an autobiography or a political essay. This book has other aims. For the last eight years I served as Spanish Prime Minister: two terms of intense political involvement, during which I tackled important national and international issues and, ultimately, was responsible for making decisions that affect us all. At the end of this period I stepped down from my post as Head of State and gradually withdrew from public life. So naturally these past few months have been filled with goodbyes as well as with reflection on the most pressing issues of my political career.

Now, therefore, seemed like a good time to put together some critical observations that sum up my opinions on some of the issues that have concerned me and will continue to concern all Spaniards for many years to come.

With that in mind, I spent a few months making tapes to record information about the circumstances I've found myself in. My good friend José María Marco has been invaluable in helping me to go over the recordings, put them in a logical order, and polish my writing. He is an excellent writer and an accomplished historian and I am deeply grateful for his professionalism, his interest, and his patience.

Given the way that this book was put together, I ask readers to be patient if they stumble over the spontaneity of the prose; that's a natural and inherent part of oral expression.

I am conscious of the fact that some journalists and some politicians reject my opinions and perspectives with a vehemence that goes far beyond mere discrepancy. So I can already imagine the kinds of reactions that this book will receive. But in spite of what some people may think, I am certainly not trying to provoke those reactions in people who will, without me to focus on, live without so much daily tension. As far as I am concerned, being a citizen means having the right to express your opinions freely. Since the very public character of my career has been stressed for what is now quite some time, I also feel obliged to express my views on the public issues concerning my country.

Readers will see that, at the end of this stage in my life, I am still passionate about Spain. That is the only reason I decided to write this book. I might use different angles, might look at issues from several vantage points, but it is always with the intention of figuring out how to improve the lives of Spaniards. Spain is a great country. It has history, constancy, and potential. Some people are tempted to destroy our unity; this does not bother me out of a conviction of absolute principles. No. To me, it's more a matter of seeing that Spaniards have accomplished great things throughout history when we worked together. Those who disagree should be judged less harshly than those who are only looking for a quick fix, pacifying their troops or, more commonly, those who don't know what they're looking for because they have no real understanding of the situation. I've often said that I hate frivolity. In life, it is detestable, and in politics it is intolerable. Spaniards deserve more than fireworks shot off in any direction, with no attention paid to what may happen when they land.

Spain's future is secure. I think I can say that I have contributed modestly to the country's current situation. I will continue to do so, to the extent possible. I would never forgive myself for not doing so, from wherever it is I may be.

CHAPTER ONE

Freedom and Leadership

I'm a liberal; I always have been. A conservative liberal, yes, but a liberal nonetheless. This can be seen in my personal outlook, my outlook on life in general, on other people, and also in a set of basic, political, social and economic principles that I hold.

I don't necessarily believe that the world created by liberalism is a perfect world, but I don't know if it's possible to find a better one. No other system that has been attempted, none that we have seen, has managed to do a better job. In any case, free society, in the liberal sense, seems to me to be the best type of society. I will always choose a liberal society, and a free world, over any other type whose principles restrict freedom arbitrarily.

The Importance of Freedom

The limits of freedom are determined by the law; they're laid out in democracy.

There is no doubt that freedom, as a concept, predates the idea of democracy. But democracy is the best way of organizing freedom. A democratic state that ensures that the law is respected is, without a doubt, what makes freedom possible. So a liberal democracy must provide a framework to insure that power can't be exercised in a despotic or cruel manner. It requires that individual rights, such as the right to free speech, to own property, and to freedom of expression and religion, among others, be respected. But freedom, as far as I am concerned, cannot exist without democracy.

Societies that call themselves democratic but do not respect freedom are actually pseudo-democratic. Communist countries were not democratic, regardless of how much the USSR insisted that its republics were democracies. They did not respect the law, nor was their structure based on rights and freedom.

Tolerance is a key part of liberalism. You always have to respect others' opinions. Politics teaches us a lot about this. The government is a permanent exercise in tolerance, although on more than one occasion it has seemed more like an exercise in patience. But tolerance, particularly in modern societies, runs the risk of going hand in hand with a lack of ideas and convictions.

That is a grave danger, perhaps the greatest of all. A lack of values, principles and convictions is the greatest risk there is for free and tolerant societies. You see, tolerance is really practiced when you are convinced that your ideas are right. If you have no deep conviction that your own ideas are the ones that ought to be defended, then you have only indifference and, deep down, contempt. Contempt for your own ideas as well as others', for those that contradict your own views but that others defend out of a deep sense of conviction.

Otherwise, if people have no convictions and no principles on which to base them, then what kind of tolerance are we really talking about? People always talk about difference and respecting difference, but in order for there to actually be difference, and in order for there to be respect for difference, you need values and ideas.

If those ideas and convictions don't exist, you soon end up in a state of nihilism, which holds that nothing is knowable or valuable because there is no reality, just as there is no possible way to find truth, or to convince anyone who does not already agree with you that you have sufficient grounds to avow what you're saying. Nihilism is the point at which rectification is impossible, because if you believe that nothing is real and everything is relative, there is no reason to accept that others may actually be right at a given point in time. Nihilism - the lack of values and firm beliefs – makes dialogue, respect and tolerance impossible. That is why it's so dangerous to have no values, principles or convictions.

In a free society no one can stop anyone else from hypothesizing about reality and then testing out their hypotheses. This process of attempting to prove one's beliefs, where everyone puts forward his or her propositions, endeavors to demonstrate their veracity, and some do so successfully, is what a free society must guarantee. It should do so while respecting the law on every level: in terms of knowledge, personal life and the creation of wealth. No one can claim to have a monopoly on knowledge. Karl Popper, author of Open Society and Its Enemies, went as far as to say that certain truth is unattainable. For that very reason, we must be open to criticism, especially in our attempts to prove what we hold to be true.

Now, a tolerant society does not have to be a skeptical one, nor one lacking in values and principles, one where what is politically correct comes to be defined by not believing or thinking or expressing opinions about anything. Nor does it have to be a kingdom of crudeness and vulgarity, where anything goes in the aim of making oneself heard, and where whoever shouts loudest grabs the public's attention. The most open, most tolerant, free societies are those that prove that their strength is inspired by values, principles and ideas that they believe in and are able to defend.

These societies are also the best able to defend themselves against a phenomenon like terrorism. In Spain we've been doing it for a long time, since the Sixties. Some countries have barely been forced to confront it, although, unfortunately, these days, no modern society is free of terrorism. Nevertheless, when faced with combating the attraction of fundamentalism and fanaticism, societies with strong beliefs, those with rock-solid values, are in a better position than those lacking them.

You have to have the courage to defend the values and ideas that you believe in. If you believe in your country, you have to say so. If you believe in a certain policy, you have to defend it, and if you are able to enact it, then you must. I, for one, have always thought that politics isn't about giving the best speeches but about undertaking the best actions. After all, it is the acts that will determine how your conduct is judged. And politics is about action, about creation.

Obviously, actions have something to back them up, a basis on which they're founded. So since having come to office in 1996, we, the Popular Party, have not made any decisions that were not well thought out; we have never improvised as we went along. Everything we've done has been carefully planned. There are probably some people who would have preferred us to deal with issues differently, or to act faster or slower on occasion, but making those choices well determines political success or failure. The key to successful politics lies in knowing how to choose your moments, how to make the right decisions and how to combine the time factor with the decision factor in such a way that the country reaps the rewards.

We believe in the historical continuity of the nation. Former Prime Minister Antonio Cánovas expressed the aim of politics quite well when he said that he was there to continue the history of Spain. So are we. And continuity requires a clear idea of your country, as well as a firm belief in it. But there's also another point, one that I think that Cánovas, too, would have agreed with. We are all a product of our time, even politicians, and that is really the only thing that guarantees continuity. Otherwise, nothing can be continued, and the actions and attitudes expressed have no basis in reality.

That is the crux of political action. We wanted a government that intervened as little as possible and a society that was as strong as possible, one that could make its own decisions. That is the reason behind our cultural initiatives, the economic support we have given to families, giving them more resources, more freedom of choice and decision-making powers. That is also why we took measures to reduce the burden on the public sector by promoting patronage and cooperation. And measures aimed at valuing initiative, merit and hard work. When you encourage those values and attitudes, you promote a society that is more open and free, and at the same time more integrated, more interconnected. The more responsibilities society assumes, the more it pulls together.

Societies that practice this sort of politics are strong societies. I'd like to think that over these past years, Spanish society has been become stronger, even if there is still some way to go. But if it has become stronger, it's because we have advanced by taking on greater personal autonomy, more responsibility, with less interventionism and less state control. More society, in short.

It's true that not everyone wants responsibilities. They are frightening; they require hard work and sacrifice. Besides, there are always others who will take them on. But sometimes it's difficult to defend the values seen in Europe today. European societies tend to be skeptical. They don't want to take on responsibilities. They don't want any risks and would rather make excuses than find a way to tackle their problems. They've retreated into a world of comfort. But without a solid foundation, those societies will erode; they won't even be able to brave a cold wind.

Family

Family is one of the greatest means of assuring strength, solidarity and cohesion in any society. This has been particularly true in Spain as a whole, in the past as well as today. During bad times, especially when the economy was stagnant, the family proved invaluable in helping people face unemployment and in giving people another chance to get ahead. In Spain, families have always known how to come through in times of trouble, when commitment and solidarity are put to the test. Who knows what would have happened without the aid of the family when, for example, 25% of the active population was unemployed, as was the case in the mid-90s.

Times have changed, and we must learn how to confront new problems arising from new situations. Spain is considerably more prosperous now than it was a few years ago. This new prosperity should not make us more selfish, nor should we be afraid to talk about the importance and the basis of the family. Obviously, we have to be open to new social realities. We cannot deny that there are situations we had not encountered up until now. The number of single-parent families has increased, families have fewer children or have them later, and they care for older family members for a longer time. The family itself seems more fragile, less stable than it was. But the fact that there are new situations and new problems is precisely why I am convinced that defending the principles that the family is based on is a worthwhile aim.

One of the things that struck me the most over the past couple of years was the considerable number of deaths that occurred in France in the summer of 2003, as a result of the heat wave. But more than that, it was the number of unclaimed dead. It's possible that some of the people who died actually had no living relatives. But what about the rest? Can people be so detached from any sort of ties that they just leave their dead family members in the hands of the state?

It's always a good idea to ask, from a government standpoint, what else can we do to strengthen the family. The first thing is to talk about it, defend it, make the case that a stable family is good for society and something that we have to take care of, to safeguard. In addition to that, we have to make policies that favor families, to the degree possible. They don't necessarily have to be policies that focus directly on families, like direct aid and financial aid. When overall taxes are lowered, that favors families because they get back funds that the state was taking away. When you give them the freedom to choose the school their kids attend, you are helping to make them stronger. When policies that lower interest rates on mortgages are put in place, you are providing them with a means of home ownership. And helping women enter into the workforce is also a means of helping families: it provides an additional source of income, gives women autonomy and a sense of self, and provides an opportunity to contribute to the betterment of society.

It's important to realize that the idea of family rests upon a notion of values, of moral principles. That lies at the heart of the matter. And that is why, although tax relief and financial assistance may be required, it can't all be reduced to that. When the family is at stake, you need values that go above and beyond a purely economic level.

Responsibility for the family is not something that can be delegated to anyone, and it certainly can't be passed on to the state. It is incumbent upon parents to exercise their responsibility if they want their children to respect them. Respect, of course, must be mutual, but responsibility is the parents' domain and in order to gain respect they must exercise it. If they don't, they won't earn their children's respect now, and later on in life their children will not respect the values that a free society is based on. Family, with everything it entails in terms of taking on responsibilities and learning respect, is part of the bedrock of freedom. It is the institution that guarantees the survival and the transmission of basic civic virtue.

Education

When we came to power, the problem of providing universal education had already been solved. All students were required to attend school to the age of 16. The previous government took care of that. We faced a different problem: the quality of that education.

We had discovered that basic knowledge in certain crucial subjects was seriously lacking, and that had to be rectified because the state must guarantee that all students leave school with an acceptable level of basic common knowledge. Really, that had been the whole point of providing universal education to begin with.

We also had to face another problem: motivation, both student and teacher. The motivation crisis hits in every country, and we decided it was time to tackle it. It was clear that teachers needed back up both in terms of authority and prestige. Not only did they need it in order to be able to do their jobs, they also deserved it, because having to work in conditions where they lacked authority and prestige, as was the case in many schools, was utterly inexcusable. As for the students, the motivation problem was different. We had to get back to reality: students had to be required to prove that they possessed certain skills in order to progress through the system.

Those were the basic tenets of our education policy. The educational authority of the Autonomous Communities was another issue. We granted educational authority to the Autonomous Communities, but at the same time, we had to maintain a certain degree of unity in a decentralized educational system. This was the determining factor in setting out the framework of all of our education-related decisions.

During my last term in office, starting in the year 2000, the educational system was completely overhauled, top to bottom. This was vital, and most families, teachers and education professionals enthusiastically accepted it. The majority knew that the old system was not working and that it was detrimental to the field, to the teaching practice, to students' futures and to Spanish society as a whole, since the price to pay for an inefficient system would be high.

But we weren't just facing problems directly related to these failures. We also had to keep other factors in mind. Because educational reform can have ideological implications, can raise issues on dangerous ground that may prove disadvantageous to everyone. So the first thing we had to do was defuse the public versus private debate; those have always been the terms of debate over education in Spain. And it's always struck me as absurd, nonsensical, particularly once education was universalized. When the public versus private debate rears its head, the only thing that ever comes as a result of it is a stampede from the public to the private sector, which ends up leaving public schools in an even worse situation than they had been before.

In addition to that, we had a historical bias working against us. Education was traditionally seen as a field pertaining to the left. The left, in fact, had a monopoly on education. How was the Popular Party going to take the country's education seriously when that was something out of our realm? Obviously, they didn't want us making any changes.

Well, our educational reforms have been extraordinarily ambitious, and as comprehensive as possible. We put the most stress on the most pressing issues. And I think that overall, Spanish society has accepted the changes introduced in quite a normal, natural way, and this shows how necessary they were. But our changes never had any ideological component. You can't play politics with Math; you can't play politics with Literature, or with humanities in general. And you must not do it with History and Geography. People might argue over some of the content, but I think it's obvious – and I thought so at the time, too – that it was time to do something about the extremes that we had come to. For example, studying local issues while ignoring the importance of gaining a general perspective on things.

The Popular Party was so convinced of this that in our first term, when we didn't have an absolute majority and Esperanza Aguirre was Education Minister, we proposed restructuring the Humanities, even though we knew we were going to lose. I remember the day perfectly. The choice we were faced with was, either withdraw the plan or lose the vote. We lost the vote in parliament, but we won a majority in the country, because the majority was in favor with what we were proposing. In fact, we passed the reform a year later. The opposition was against it and I'm convinced it was a serious miscalculation on their part.

For us, it was a very conscious decision. It was what had to be done, something completely logical. In the same way that it's just common sense that if you tell teachers that they have to work for their prestige and earn respect on a daily basis you also have to support them, it was common sense to require students to learn the country's geography in addition to their town's geography, and to know who Cervantes and Quevedo and Góngora were, for example.

Once education is universalized, it's also perfectly logical to introduce a means of rewarding effort and hard work through performance-based pay. And to offer students different opportunities. Not everyone will want to go to college; some will choose other paths. That's why we have Vocational Training, which provides students with a whole range of possibilities, giving them the quality preparation needed for a wide variety of jobs.

Of course, some students simply don't want to finish school. In that case, you have two choices. You can force them to keep going, thereby creating a negative environment for the rest of the class, or you can allow them to enter the workforce, making sure they have the minimum training that everyone should posses and keeping in mind that they can always go back to school later on if they so choose.

If you take the first option, you end up degrading education, because you stop requiring anyone to follow even the most basic rules of common courtesy and cooperation, thereby disrespecting both students and teachers. If in addition to that you don't require any level of basic knowledge to be proven, don't demand that students work in order to pass on to the next grade – which is what had been happening – then you end up with a system that is a complete failure.

Education in this country had reached such levels of absurdity that, for example, parents would turn up at a school that had no principal, because no one wanted to be principal, and just try to talk to anyone they could find, to determine whether their kids were learning anything or not. Because from their grades it was impossible to tell. Things couldn't go on like that.

The Quality of Education Act, put forth when Pilar del Castillo was Education Minister, has made great strides: each teacher takes responsibility for grading in his or her own subject; we have reintroduced exams; we have made it possible to ensure better behavior in the classroom; and we have put an end to automatically passing students from one grade to the next, amongst other things. We have also made great strides in providing resources for grants and scholarships, for university reforms and for research funds. The reforms needed to improve the quality of high school education were so obvious that there really should have been no debate over them.

Entrepreneurial Spirit

Until quite recently, Spain's market economy had bad press. When I started my political career, people used to say that you shouldn't have meetings with business leaders, especially in small towns where everybody would find out what you were doing. Business meetings were bad, business was bad and businesspeople were almost seen as evil.

Things have changed a lot since then. Now there are many people working in business and finance. Where once there was only one business school, if that, now there are several; and there are publishers and specialized subjects. People are making a considerable intellectual effort. People have worked hard and it shows. For those of us who have always defended a market economy and always known that entrepreneurial initiative is the driving force behind an economy, and therefore a company, this is great progress. The more companies there are in a country, the better off it is, and the same goes for businesspeople. I think there has been a huge change in people's mindset.

Businesspeople themselves, no doubt, have largely contributed to this change. The over four million jobs that have been created in the past few years have been created by business. That means that there are more freelancers, more industrialists, and more executives willing not only to create start-ups but also to hire people and take on the considerable responsibilities that that entails. That changes people's outlook. And generally speaking, there has been a positive response to the challenge of awarding entrepreneurial activity and the market economy the prestige they deserve.

Here in Spain, more and more people want to be independent. They are beginning to show the sort of initiative that tends to develop into an entrepreneurial spirit. There are now many people who prefer working for themselves than being employed by others, in spite of the inherent risks. That is great for the country.

The government can and should help them. In order to do so, it must provide a secure, stable framework, one that is as flexible as possible so as to make start-ups, job creation and contracting attractive. For example, my government got rid of the Economic Activity Tax. It was an absurd hindrance. Anyone who is self-employed will tell you, "I understand why I am taxed if I have benefits; I'd prefer not to be taxed highly, but I understand. What is incomprehensible is that I am taxed merely for wanting to be self-employed and start my own company." That is a surefire way to discourage the creation of wealth and job creation.

The same is true of pension funds and savings. The Popular Party encouraged capital mobility, and I'm convinced that that was one of the best things we did in the first term. Measures like that are the reason that Spain is now the European country that receives the most financial investment, and those investments can then be distributed from here to other countries.

Spain's commercial framework is tightly woven, especially in small- to medium-sized businesses. They are dynamic and they create a lot of employment, but they also have to face specific problems. For example, it takes longer for them to adapt to changing technology. But it's clear that they have made progress. You can tell by investment levels and by the sheer number of businesses created over the past few years. They have taken on business and investment risks both domestically and internationally. And making the country attractive to foreign investors has forced Spanish businesspeople to get a move on in order to survive.

Business executives also know that there are union spokespeople who will take on national roles in an attempt to negotiate and reach agreements, and who are well regarded and valued by the government as important components for the progress of the country as a whole.

If businesspeople are given a stable framework and security measures, and if steps are taken to stimulate activity instead of hindering it, then you can be sure of business growth. It's not like it used to be. Now, one of the first things that anyone wanting to enter the political arena needs to do is sit down and talk to the business leaders. That is a very important, very positive sign of change.

Institutional Stability

A strong country needs strong institutions. Spain has them, but it also needs to ensure smooth running and stability for the future; it needs to make sure that there are no sudden surprises, that no cracks appear. Of course there will always be good times and more difficult ones, that is only natural; making certain that the country's institutions all function properly is what's really important.

When I realized that, I thought that one of the ways I could contribute to institutional stability was through a commitment to a limited term of office. Another way is to make sure that terms run for the established period, which is four years, out of respect for the institutions themselves and because teams have to be formed, people have to get settled in, policies have to be put into practice and all of that takes time. It seems like four years, the duration of a term, is a long time, but it's not.

A third way to contribute to institutional stability is to accept and honor parliamentary control. Over the past eight years, I have answered more parliamentary questions than all the rest of Spain's democratic Prime Ministers put together. Parliamentary control is vital, it is one of the central tenets of parliamentary life and that's a good thing.

There are a few truisms as far as Parliament is concerned. Sometimes it seems as if Parliament runs based not on what voters have decided is right and desirable, and thus elected via a majority, but based on what the electorate has rejected, on the ideas of those whom voters have not chosen to enact their politics. Some people think that what is reasonable in Parliament is that the majority always compromise for the sake of the minority, accepting the latter's postulates. Now, it's obvious that politicians should never legislate against anyone; minorities must be respected and to the degree that it's valuable, it's a good idea to reach the widest agreements possible. Having said that, what is reasonable in Parliament is that the majority rule, because that's why voters put them there to begin with. That's what the people wanted. If they had wanted something else, there would have been a different majority, a different party in power and a different platform.

We established very important control mechanisms. In addition to having the government appear weekly before Parliament, candidates for posts chosen by Parliament must also appear. These candidates have to report and clarify their projects and ideas. We've changed a lot of things, for the better, I think. Perhaps, from a parliamentary perspective, it would be worth amending some things, like certain debates. For example, budget debates are always excessively tedious and long-winded. They open a huge gulf between the government and the people.

We decided to keep the State of the Nation debate. It has become a tradition, a custom, and that has to be respected. All Parliamentary debates end up as some sort of public duel and this one is certainly no exception. The way it is currently set up, it requires incredible stamina and considerable rhetorical skill. I recall debates in which I spent nine hours straight in the Plenary Hall, nonstop, and then had to get up and do it again the next day.

But the effort has its rewards, and debates are a useful way to outline proposals, bring them to light and find out what others think of them. Personally, I enjoy expounding and refuting; I think that's clear. I also, however, think it's important that when we debate, we do it about real issues. I recall one State of the Nation debate where I actually heard the new opposition leader pose the issue of the anniversary of the publication of Don Quijote – twice – as if it were a matter of life and death. He wanted to know if we were going to celebrate 2005 as the Year of Cervantes. Needless to say, I was dumbfounded.

The Media's Manipulation of Spanish Reality

Everyone, in the course of his or her life, lives through an earth-shattering historical event. For us it was the Prestige oil tanker disaster, which was Spain's first ecological media event. Never before had an environmental catastrophe been on live broadcast in this country. And it went to some shocking extremes. Fervor and political designs were given free reign. Of course, people showed a great and important interest in the informative aspect of the tragedy. But some also wanted to turn it into an opportunity for political gain, not just for economic gain.

Something similar happens in the media as a whole. I have some reservations about the media's general tone. I've said it before and I'll keep saying it. I am convinced that if those in charge of the networks were more interested in making television reflect the reality of the country, they might be surprised; they might be more successful than they think.

Right now, everything on television has the same tone. The channels all show the same kinds of shows, and they all want to push the boat out, go as far as possible. I think that in some areas, there should be some ground rules, so to speak. But of course, only those in charge of the stations can lay down those rules. Obviously, no one is going to censor them in any way, because people are free to produce, broadcast, or watch whatever they want. It has to be the entrepreneurs themselves who set the limits, who make it clear that in their business you just don't say certain things about people, you don't exalt marginal behavior and make a show of it. That doesn't limit anyone's freedom of expression.

It is legitimate, yes, for the head of a radio or television station, or some form of media, someone whose role includes programming decisions, to try to reap the maximum benefits for his or her company. And that is accomplished by entertaining the maximum number of people and, thus, obtaining the largest audience or listenership. But I cannot see how that goes against the idea of maintaining some semblance of quality control. In fact, just the opposite. It would appear that these days, what is normal on television is most definitely not normal for the majority. Obscenity, uproar, constant insults…these are not part of most people's everyday lives. No doubt it attracts an audience, because anything attracts an audience. But those viewers do not represent the entire population, nor does everyone have to accept the same criteria. I am personally convinced that there are very clear managerial and commercial responsibilities that need to be exercised here.

When television transmits information, it simplifies things so that a majority of the people can understand them. But there is a big difference between simplifying things and making them vulgar, or having a majority of programs be about the same thing, as happens on certain nights. I have actually been asked to step in and do something about this. But that makes no sense. If this is truly a free society, then it has to be the heads of programming or station directors themselves who decide to impose limits.

This is probably more than a general questioning of the overall tone of many programs. There are always, of course, marginal subjects, but they have little bearing on the general population's interests or on their lives. It's fine to deal with marginal subjects, as long as they are seen for what they are. But exalting them is a very different thing; there is no reason to act as if society as a whole should be concerned with it. We end up in a paradox: it turns out that what is actually normal for vast majority of the population is seen as strange and trivial.

The intellectual world in Spain, generally speaking, has taken quite a long time to accept and take on board certain pressing historical and political obligations. I'm talking about taking action against terrorism, or in favor of free and peaceful living in some parts of the country. It is curious to see how readily opinions – albeit legitimate – are put forth against our foreign policy, for example, and yet when it comes to defending our freedom and our basic right to life as threatened by terrorism, there is near silence. It's true that this has changed over time. Society as a whole had already accepted these responsibilities and little by little, the distance between the intellectual world and Spanish society is being bridged.

But in the media, it seems as if things have gone the other way and the distance is actually increasing. Here, the problem is that there are important ideas and opinions that could be extraordinarily useful to society, that could lead the way, but they are either sidelined or they receive less consideration than they should. And this is not because they are not expressed or are unreliable. It is simply that there are other issues that take center stage and get the media's attention. This is a serious problem in our society.

Nevertheless, it has been proven that when you take the public seriously, they respond. There have been historical studies, biographies, and some studies that uncover new findings about Spain's past that have become great successes in publishing. So have some works of fiction based on our country's history. We have an extraordinarily rich cultural history, full of events that could be of great interest to the public. They are there, waiting for someone to take advantage of them, in a respectful and imaginative way; they don't have to be distorted in any way, not the events themselves or the values they represent. There are plenty of opportunities around for people who want to make use of them, and know how to do it properly.

The same could be said of our current affairs. I don't know why no one makes movies or writes novels about what is going on right now in the Basque Country. For example, one man was sent a key to his own house with the warning that they had more; a councilor at city hall was forced to sit beside someone whom he knew had denounced a friend of his who was murdered; an ETA member was ordered by the organization to murder a man who had saved his life when they were kids…These are testimonies to personal freedom of immeasurable value. They could teach us about commitment and the heroism of so many people who are permanently subjected to terror and harassment. I have been trying to get someone to make films about these events for years. I've even begged. But so far to no avail, I'm afraid.

Spanish Culture

For the past eight years I've had the Republican Presidential Battalion flag in my office; it belonged to Manuel Azaña, leader of Spain's Second Republic. I would have liked to donate it to the Museum of the Armed Forces in Toledo at the end of my term, but since the museum is still under construction, it will have to wait. My possession of the flag stems from a conversation I had with José Barrionuevo after the launch of Federico Jiménez Losantos' book on Azaña. Barrionuevo told me that he had managed to get hold of Azaña's presidential flag and had given it to former Prime Minister Felipe González.

When I started my term as Prime Minister, there were no documents and there was no flag in Moncloa Palace. I mentioned this to Adolfo Suárez, who must have arranged something, because not long thereafter González sent the flag to me, with a card. I've kept it in my office all these years and I want to return it, now, to the Armed Forces. It doesn't make much sense for me to hold onto it, after all.

One of my happiest moments during these years was the inauguration of the newly remodeled Italian paintings collection rooms in the Prado Museum. I've always thought that the Prado is the most important thing in Spain. It is a symbol of Spain's cultural contribution to the world; that's why it is so important. Given my belief on the matter, what starts off as a personal conviction becomes a political and moral obligation for someone in office.

I am personally very pleased to have helped make it possible for the Prado be able to undergo some much-needed upgrades and improvements. When the Popular Party came to power, the Prado was in need of some serious attention. There was no room to store collections or even to keep the archives in order. All that has changed. The building has been modernized, problems have been rectified, and additional collections have been placed, such as the sculpture collection which was previously not on display. And then they began work on the Italian rooms, which was carried out beautifully. The Prado also underwent extensive expansion, as did the Reina Sofía Museum.

There were a lot of obstacles to overcome, a lot of problems to solve. I wanted to restore the King's Hall, which is almost all that is left of the Palace of the Buen Retiro, and to reopen it to the public so that people could see it as it was during the reign of King Philip IV. This was the place where the Catholic Monarchy – the Spanish monarchy - displayed its symbols. It summed up the political and cultural enterprise of Golden Age Spain. This is something well worth regaining, explaining, and showing to the public.

Now, the building that houses the Kings' Hall is also where the Army Museum is. The Army Museum is one of Spain's great museums and one of the most important army museums in the world, but it used to receive very few visitors. It needed a new significance; it had to become a place that explained the history of Spain through its armies. Not just the country's military history, which of course is vital, but the entire history of the nation via the actions and the national and global commitment of its army. The best way to do this was to move the museum to another location, and the Toledo Fortress was the best place.

More people were visiting the Fortress than the Army Museum as it was. Since Toledo is close to Madrid, moving the museum also helps revitalize the city, which has changed a lot in the past few years. And, since it is Charles V's old palace, it is the best imaginable headquarters for a Museum of Spanish History told via the Armed Forces.

This was a very complicated project, requiring a near-complete restructuring of the Prado, moving the Army Museum collection, which is amazing but can be very difficult to move, and setting up a new museum. There was a lot of resistance, of course, and some of it was understandable. But I was not prepared to let anything stand in the way, just as I didn't let anything get in the way of the Prado and Reina Sofía expansions. I had to act forcefully, to show that there was no going back; that was the only way to get the message across. With the Prado I've been pushing nonstop since 1996, without a break.

Teaching a country's history is vital. It is absolutely fundamental that people know not only what happened but why; they need to know where they come from, what their elders did over the years, how the society we live in was created, how the customs and values we hold took shape. People have a right to have their questions about the society they live in answered. That is what teaching history is all about, that is why the educational system as a whole is so meaningful; it is a vehicle for transmitting culture. One way to define culture is to see it as a means of continuing values. That's why the Ministry of Culture and Education is one and the same.

Since Spain is a very decentralized country, especially when it comes to education, different regions teach their own histories, and sometimes make up stories aimed at reinforcing a particular sense of identity. But if the history of Spain, of the country, is not also taught, if we don't transmit the values and the great works that make up Spanish culture, then there is no way to contest those invented histories.

How many people in Spain today actually know that Basque explorer Legazpi was the navigator who traveled to the Philippines and founded Manila? We hope the answer is lots, which is why we put on a Legazpi exhibition that opened at the end of 2003. We wanted to bring to the fore the global dimension of Spanish history and culture; this global dimension was a vital contribution to the progress of humanity, and we felt it was important to explain the Basque contribution. But Legazpi is just a part of that contribution. We could also talk about Basque industrialists, and the Basque civil servants at the service of the Spanish Crown, and the roles of many Basques as Secretary of State.

I tried to do this type of work in Castilla y León, too. When I came into power, there were discussions about which city in Castilla y León should host the Autonomous Community's celebrations and which city should be seat of the local government. That's an indicator of how far off track things had gotten. We wanted to give them back a clear sense of their historical importance, and at the same time modernize the Autonomy, so it was in step with the times.

My government's first task in this area was to help recover the country's cultural and historical heritage, which in Spain's case is extraordinarily rich. Then, of course, came the issue of using all possible resources to promote it. And that's what we did. For example, we held exhibitions on the important ex Prime Ministers Cánovas and Sagasta, on the Cortes - or Spanish Parliament - and on the monarchy (Philip V, Philip II, Charles V) in the Senate collections; we also had an exhibit on the history of Jews in Spain - called "Memory of Sefarad" - and there will be one to commemorate the anniversary of Isabel, the Catholic Queen. We have also put on numerous cultural functions and exhibits celebrating the works of Federico García Lorca, Luis Cernuda, Max Aub and the 500 year anniversary of the birth of Garcilaso de la Vega. National museums, particularly the Reina Sofía, have also done a lot to keep bringing 20th-century artists, who sometimes lay forgotten, to the fore.

I have never seen Spain as a problem. I have seen problematic Spaniards, which is not the same thing. But Spain as a problem? Never. The worst thing about the Black Legend that was spread about Spaniards is not that it was popular in other countries. That happens every time a country becomes a hegemonic power. But other countries don't usually believe it.

We believed it. When Spain went through hard times, when the empire went into decline, we used the Black Legend as a means of historical introspection. We started to ask ourselves: what is Spain? Is Spain a problem? What is our problem? Are we exceptional, different from other countries?

That's a waste of time and effort. It's a type of self-obsession and questioning that leads only to frustration. Spain is not a problem in and of itself; it never has been. Spain has problems, just like every other country. Italy has its problems; France has its problems; Germany, the United Kingdom and the United States all have their problems. But no one in those countries suggests that the country is the problem. Our basic problem is that some people want to destroy the country. That is a serious problem that we are facing, but it doesn't mean that Spain as a nation is a problem in and of itself.

Moreover, in spite of all that has been said and done, we have always survived, we have always bounced back and we have always come out ahead. The image of Spain today has changed completely and utterly. We are respected, we are reliable, and we have credibility. We are no longer a cultural exception, a country where people go to have a good time or to study a few geniuses who didn't conform to Western culture. We are integral, we have initiative and we can make our voice heard anywhere, in any international forum.

We now are the cultural power that it was always our mission to be. For example, book publishing since 1996 has increased tremendously; people are going to the movies much more regularly; theaters are making more money from plays; there has been an upsurge in the number of concerts performed. Culture is our greatest asset as a country. We are known and renowned for our culture all over the world, and our culture is a manifestation of our wealth and diversity; it's a way to be open, innovative, and tolerant. It is a reflection of who we are, of our aspirations and our problems, of what we are and what we want to be.

Recovering our past was a way of recovering a national feeling, one which people said had faded, although I was never convinced of that. We made an effort to explain Spanish history this way. Another example of this is how much care is given to our archives, including making the National Archives available online.

I created the Cultural Affairs Commission, which is presided over by the Prime Minister and which a majority of cabinet ministers are part of. It was important for the whole administration to take part in recovering and reevaluating our culture. I'm proud of the work I did in this area. We wanted to help, to promote Spanish culture and to encourage it, showing equal regard for all political standpoints. We didn't choose which past we wanted to represent based on political ideology; there were no political agendas here.

We have to be able to talk about our culture without getting into shouting matches, like normal human beings. We need to get rid of our historical complex. We have to use discretion, make sure not to overwhelm people. We are too old and too strong a country and a culture to be going around vindicating anything now. But we must also not exclude anything or anyone. We're not going to vindicate any exclusive, monolithic identity. We want to be positive, to talk about everybody's contributions. But we also have to do without an inferiority complex, without feeling unworthy, because all we're doing is telling the truth. And because that's what people know, and feel, and need someone in public office to say.

Culture in Spanish

With those aims in mind, we've tried to advance Spanish culture abroad, as well as promote artistic and intellectual creation here in Spain. We've helped artists and creators, encouraged artistic production and created several institutions to help publicize our artists and creators abroad. We've put new bodies in charge, like SEACEX (State Society for Cultural Action Abroad) and also tried to use those that already existed. And the great success that the cultural functions and exhibitions organized abroad have had is testament to the fact that this is a great moment for Spanish artistic creation.

Here is something true of Spanish culture that can only be said of great cultures: it has nothing to fear from globalization. Quite the opposite, in fact. Globalization underpins it. Globalization, after all, is first and foremost universalization and Spanish culture has a strong universal calling. Besides, Spain was already a globalizing force in the 16th and 17th centuries, and kept it up until the 19th century. And that globalization went hand in hand with cultural components that survived even after the political structures that originally sustained them disappeared. I'm talking about a wide variety of cultural components, but one, in particular, is the most valuable: the Spanish language.

I have a vivid memory of my visit to Cuzco, because in Cuzco it becomes immediately clear what the Spanish presence in America meant. In terms of realizing the extent of the Spanish dimension in

America, though, my greatest surprise came somewhere else. During a visit to Bolivia, the President took me to Concepción, his hometown. It's a town of some three thousand inhabitants, on the banks of the Amazon. We landed in a field and then went to a religious ceremony in a church. The church was full of Bolivian Indians, and I found out that the bishop presiding over the ceremony was Bulgarian, though, of course, he was speaking Spanish. When we were walking through the church, the bishop said, "Turn around and look up." I did, and there I saw, presiding over the church, the coat of arms of Asturias. There was also a children's choir singing baroque music. They had preserved 18th century instruments, and they sang in Spanish and played the music that had first been played over two hundred years ago.

If I had to pick one incident from the first years of Spanish presence in America, I'd choose Hernán Cortés in Mexico. His arrival, seeing the Aztec city of Tenochtitlán for the first time, his relationship with Moctezuma, and then Noche Triste, the sad night when those men cried, believing that all was lost. It is absolutely fascinating, and some of the figures who took part in the events and changed the direction of history, like Cortés did, are truly colossal. They are also polemical, of course, but an event of that magnitude always is; otherwise it wouldn't be so spectacular and wouldn't carry such weight.

Octavio Paz said that when Cortés stopped being a myth and became what he really is, a historical character, then Mexicans would finally be able to see themselves clearly. That is what I find so fascinating about Cortés: the historical figure, not the symbol. His arrival, his first contact, his energy. Mexican historiography has already sorted out the legend from the man and revealed the real Cortés in biographies by José Luis Martínez and Juan Miralles.

So in a way, the moment Octavio Paz was waiting for has probably already come to pass. Mexico is an important country, a great, reliable nation capable of taking a lead role in coordinating efforts in Latin America and of brokering treaties with North American countries, too. They have taken serious action to ensure democratic stability and shown a desire to modernize economically. And Mexico has also generated some vehicles for cultural dialogue that span both sides of the Atlantic, such as the magazine Vuelta, which now comes out of Spain and is called Letras Libres. That is just one example of the important cultural contribution Mexico makes to the wide range of voices that make up the Ibero-American community and culture in Spanish.

The last time I was in Florida, I went to Tallahassee, the state capital, located far north of what we associate with Florida, which is Miami and the southern part of the state. Governor Jeb Bush, the President's brother, told me on that trip that it was our fault, Spaniards' fault, that that's where the capital was. "What do you mean, our fault?" I asked. He explained that the Spanish had chosen Tallahassee as capital because it was halfway between Saint Augustine and Pensacola. So it's because of the Spaniards' strategic decision that Tallahassee is the state capital.

I also learned some other very interesting news on that trip. We are still fifty years away from the time when Americans can say that the US flag has been flying over Florida longer than the flag of the Spanish Crown did. If you keep in mind that a large part of North America once belonged to the Spanish Crown, then it's clear that we have something in common with the current population of the United States: the recent Latino influx into the US, its relevance, its impact and vitality, and the fact that Latinos are integrating into US society without losing their own culture and language.

This all makes for a world that not only is Spanish, but that expresses itself in Spanish, a world in Spanish. And when that world stops to think about its roots, those roots will be in Spanish. Spain must be present. We have to keep making institutional efforts to spread the language and to help the culture stay alive.

In my last two terms the Cervantes Institute, which is one of the most important associations for the teaching of the Spanish language and promoting Spanish culture abroad, and which has over fifty centers around the world, has continued to see its number of students steadily and dramatically increase each year. Its success is a direct result of the desire to learn Spanish that we are seeing all over the world, from Far East countries like South Korea and Vietnam, to the Middle East, and from North Africa to our European neighbors. And people's interest is not limited to the language; more and more, we are seeing an international interest in culture and in the doors that open when you speak a language spoken by 400 million people.

In the year 2000 we created the Carolina Foundation, an institution in charge of cultural relations and educational cooperation, particularly with Latin American countries. The Foundation is entrusted with two important programs, one that provides grants for continuing education and one for visiting scholars. The latter is aimed at allowing people to come from abroad and spend a set period of time here, familiarizing themselves with our culture and making contacts with the most distinguished researchers in their fields here. Both programs help Spain internationally, by establishing links and creating a way to share experiences.

We have no desire to impose any unilateral vision. The whole world in Spanish is infinitely diverse. In Argentina, in Chile, in Colombia and in Guatemala it's diverse, but also in Brazil, where people study Spanish as a second language as a matter of course. The world that makes up the world in Spanish comes from vastly different backgrounds and has vastly different experiences. Those who have immigrated to the US have different sorts of issues, because they are integrating into a different culture. They numbered 37 million in 2001 and it's estimated that by 2015 they will number 50 million. But not only are the numbers on the rise; their influence, too, continues to grow and will keep growing.

All these people will eventually become part of a culture that is Anglo-Saxon in origin. But they also have roots that tie them to another part of Europe, thanks to their Hispanic heritage. This is the legacy of our language, the legacy of the Peruvian Inca Garcilaso, of the Argentinean Sarmiento and of Cuban Lezama Lima, just as it is the legacy of Spaniards like Galdós, Lope de Vega and Cervantes. And this legacy, clearly, has repercussions as far as Spain's commitments and political actions abroad. That's a reality we can't ignore. We can't pretend that the almost 40 million North Americans who speak Spanish don't exist. Their existence is not just an advantage. It's a responsibility.

Leadership

Leadership requires conviction and decisiveness. In order to truly act as a leader you need a combination of strong convictions and decision-making abilities. There are, of course, other important factors. Communication skills are indispensable in a world where you have to get through to people whose lives and circumstances vary greatly. Team building is important, and so are powers of persuasion. But convictions and decision-making abilities are at the top of the list.

The best example of leadership, the one that impresses me the most, is that of Pope John Paul II. He is a man who is entirely focused on what he needs to do, who knows what he wants to say and has the inner strength to defend it, to weather the storm; and he has the courage, ability and determination to follow through. That's why the Pope has such amazing powers of mobilization.

What we are witnessing right now is truly unique. I have never seen such powers of endurance, such a refusal to stumble and fall. And it is that tremendous strength that leads him to say, "I still have things to take care of, and I want to live so that I can do them; I'll suffer whatever it takes, but I'm not letting go."

The older you get, naturally, the more you tend to focus on what you consider truly vital. That's a good sign, because it means that you've had a lot of experience and you've learned to sideline things that don't matter, things that are really of no interest. The Pope has always gone straight to the heart of the matter and that's why he's been able to show universal leadership. He is truly incredible and admirable.

Great leaders change the world, and change it for the better, clearly. Churchill combined conviction and decisiveness to an extraordinary degree. He withstood unbelievably tough conditions while showing determination with regard to morality and his deep-seated historic ideals about the English nation. The 1940s are now used as a point of reference in Englands's history, and in world history. The British refused to bow down; they stood firm and came out ahead for it.

That was when Churchill was at the helm. But he made a mistake in not stepping down in time. He could have stepped down, proud of what he had accomplished, as the symbol of the country and of English history; he shouldn't have tried to carry on as Prime Minister after his best years, when he'd already made his most important contributions. Churchill said that great nations are ungrateful, but that was probably a reaction to his disappointment at losing the election right after the war. Really, what people were trying to tell him was that he'd already accomplished what he had to accomplish.

Leadership is shown in times when you find yourself in adverse situations and are able to stand firm with your convictions. I knew that I was facing one of those times when, even before I came to power, the Popular Party decided to stand firmly against terrorism and anyone who supported it. Once in power, I really saw the degree to which this was a matter requiring great powers of resistance that needed to be based on deep-seated moral and political convictions.

One of the problems of modern leadership is not that governments do or don't listen to the people. The problem arises when governments allow opinion polls and the interest of short-term popularity to influence policy more than their own political responsibility. Now, clearly you've got to listen to the people; no one is debating that. But then you have to have the courage to make decisions that are in the public's best interest and that come from your convictions. Decisions cannot be made based on media pressure or opinion polls. That results in a media leadership, and those are always weak because, when it comes down to it, those leaders are incapable of saying and defending what they think and are unwilling to pay the price you have to pay. I've always respected people who are willing to say and defend their beliefs, even if I disagree with them.

During the Iraq war, I did what I thought I had to do. I also saw how well the work we had already been doing for years served us. Strong leadership was valuable then, to keep the party united, to make people feel safe and to show them that they had our support. A leader must never shirk responsibilities. If you shirk your responsibilities then you can't hold others responsible for theirs. But for others to take on their own responsibilities, they have to be allowed to make mistakes, and that, too, is a sign of responsibility: knowing where to draw the line.

Some people think that a position of leadership is something that has to be treated with kid gloves, preserved, something you have to watch others do from behind the scenes for a long time before taking part. Personally, I think just the opposite. There has not been a single important government matter that I have not been at the head of. And I've been happy to be at the helm; I wouldn't want it any other way, nor could I do it any other way.

Of course, decisions have to be carefully considered. Sometimes it takes awhile to make decisions, and you have to reflect carefully and at length. When it comes to the day-to-day stuff, you can be as warm and open as you want. But that's not really necessary, nor does it obscure what is really important. People can always tell whether you're being sincere or not. Just like they can tell when you're truly enthusiastic about something. Once you make a decision, you have to stick to it. I have never had a problem with that.

Another feature of leadership is that it has to be earned. You work at it over time, every day, for years. When I took leadership of the Popular Party and was just starting to become known, they said I didn't have what it took to be a leader. Now that I am about to leave office having served as Prime Minister for eight years, they say that I am the archetypal super-leader. Neither of those things is true. The thing is, leadership takes practice. And if in the course of your leadership you achieve results that the majority consider reasonable, then it doesn't decline, it grows over time. Politics, morals and actions are all contributing factors.

That is why it's easy to tell when someone has no leadership skills. It's not hard to tell a real leader from a cardboard cut-out. Modern society, unfortunately, encourages the latter. Some people think they have what it takes to be a leader when they really don't. That's what happens when people confuse leadership with image. And that's why, in general, there are so few leaders with strong convictions in modern society.

Modern societies are open societies, diverse societies, where people have to make their own decisions as they confront new situations. Maybe they didn't used to have to make their own decisions because they followed traditions or norms. That's why it's so vital that we have points of reference, convictions – in the deepest sense of the word – to fall back on. A real leader cannot allow there to be a sense of insecurity or instability. It's important to lead the way without making people dependent. I have never encouraged dependence. Never. You have to put a limit on things, draw the line and say, "This is as far as it goes."

I'm an extrovert. At home, at least. When I'm not at home I am, perhaps, a little abrupt. Not on a personal level, nor in the political arena, but when I speak. What can I say? That's just the way I am. Like Fernando de los Ríos said to Azaña, "Don't be so brusque, don Manuel." Well, given that that's part of my personality, while I was in office people had an image of me as part authoritarian and part arrogant. I've never been concerned with images. In fact, I hate the idea of them.

When you're Prime Minister, you have to lead the country, and leading the country means making decisions that no one else can make. That's what I did. I don't think I was authoritarian and I was open to dialogue. If anyone knows of a Prime Minister who signed more agreements than me, I'd be delighted to hear about it, really.

I like to take things seriously, both personally and politically. I like direct people who say what they think and follow through. That is what dialogue is based on, after all, and that's what tolerance is based on, too. Tolerance is not about not having your own values and ideas, or about doing whatever someone wants you to do. It's about respecting the convictions of others, as I've said, without giving up your own convictions or refraining from acting on them. I like to say what I believe openly, clearly if possible, and this is something that becomes more obvious over the years. I used to really enjoy party functions. And I still do. But as the years go by, what you really want to do is say what you have to say and, if possible, get people to agree. That's the only thing that really matters. Some time ago I went to Barcelona and I started off by saying, "I'm going to tell you three things." And I did, I told them three things. First this, second that, and third the other. And now someone else will come along and do it better than me.

That's the way it is. The first time you speak in public in front of a large audience, a packed bullring for example, you walk in and it's a thrill and you like it. When you've spoken in fifty packed bullrings, it's not the same thing. I'm not looking for personal satisfaction anymore. I'm there to say what I want to say. It's enjoyable, it's important, sure. I like seeing people, greeting the people who've taken the time to attend the event, speaking to them. But the important thing is whatever reason brought you there to begin with.

Churchill said there's nothing worse than doing something halfway. I agree. You can never make a decision halfway, for either personal or political reasons. I am incapable of it. If I have a certain responsibility I see to it, and if I don't, I don't.

Deciding to Step Down

Deciding to step down is something that can't be done halfway. I decided to step down long before becoming Prime Minister. And it's a decision I've thought about every day I've been in office. Every day, I've thought about the day I'd have to leave office. It's good discipline. It protects you from temptations and reaffirms your conviction. I also made myself say it out loud and commit to it in public. A lot of people asked me not to, although most people know that I can't be pressured into anything. Lots of people told me not to even consider stepping down, people in Spain and abroad. Some even thought I was just acting, that it was a trick so I could later return amidst great fanfare.

I've never given anyone reason to think that. I have never shown any doubts. I would never say one thing in public and then later, behind closed doors, say something else. I know there are a lot of people who don't like what I've done. There are those who keep going on about it even after realizing that it was an irrevocable decision. But I've always been totally upfront about it. If I hadn't, it would have been obvious, because people can tell when you're not telling the truth, especially about something as serious as this.

I don't know if my actions will set a precedent, but I am totally convinced that I did the right thing. We'll see. I think that stepping down after eight years as Head of State was good for the stability of our political institutions, and also good for the party.

The Popular Party has behaved brilliantly. This was a very risky situation for everyone. It required a lot of discipline, required that we be sure that ours was the best platform for Spain, and required confidence and the conviction that regardless of the outcome, we were all acting in good faith. That is what was at stake when I proposed the man I thought was the best candidate for Spanish Prime Minister. It was a test – one more test – of inner strength and of the Popular Party's unity.

Mariano Rajoy is an honorable, levelheaded man with an excellent background and outstanding political experience. He is a brave man who has faced moments of crisis fearlessly. He has a clear idea of Spain and the historical and constitutional foundations that the continuity, the prosperity and the freedom of our country rest on. And as he clearly showed in September, he is a guaranteed leader within the party.

Now, I have to admit that leaving office was not necessarily the best thing for me personally. I've been doing what I enjoy most over these eight years. I will never again have access to so much information, never again have the decision-making powers that I have now. There is an insurmountable difference between being Prime Minister and holding any other public post. Here, in this office, you have a responsibility that is yours alone: you have to be there to answer for your decisions, to face your citizens, and you are the deciding factor on many issues.

It's true that there is no place to hide; you have no shelter from the storm. A cabinet minister does. You are his or her shelter. The Prime Minister has none, and you can't go looking for it because if you do, you're making a mistake. The people will know you are not a fit leader. That's the real difference. And you have to be willing to pay the price that goes with that, the solitude that goes with it. That is not true of any other office.

Having served as Prime Minister of my country is the most important, most serious aspiration I could have dreamed of. Deciding to step down after eight years was very hard, especially since carrying on would have been seen as reasonable, given my age and the general outlook.

But I am absolutely convinced that this is the best thing for my country. People might argue, and I myself agree, that I led my party well and now it's time for someone else to lead. That I made a lot of decisions and now it's time for others to decide. That it should not be personalized. But if I didn't believe that stepping down as party leader were good for both my party and my country, I would never have done it.

CHAPTER TWO

The Popular Party: A Centrist Party

I've always been interested in the news; it runs in my family. My father, Manuel Aznar Acedo, was a journalist. At home we followed politics closely. We got every newspaper there was back then, in the Seventies. I read them and I was up on current affairs, on the issues of the day, on everything that was going on. My classmates weren't as interested as I was in those things. I thought that was odd. It seemed natural to me, I thought everyone should be as interested in political affairs as I was, but they weren't.

People in my family were history buffs, too. My father inherited his interest in history from his father, my grandfather, Manuel Aznar Zubigaray, who was a journalist and author of several history books. I met him late, in 1967, when he returned to Madrid after having served as Ambassador to the United Nations. My grandfather's career path was long, and listening to him was fascinating.

When I graduated with a degree in Law from Madrid's Complutense University, I decided to get my professional career on track as fast as possible. I had already met Ana, the woman who would become my wife. And in order for us to get married, I needed a stable job. Both of us were studying for government civil service exams. Ana was studying for the exams required to become a specialist in State Civil Administration, and I was going for Tax Inspector.

This was between 1975 and 1976. In October of 1975, someone recommended a certain preparatory academy to me. So I went there and spoke to the director. I told him I wanted to get a post as Tax Inspector in one year and asked him what I'd have to do. He told me all the topics I'd have to master and I got my place in the time I'd set out to do it in. I passed my exams in December of 1976. On January 1, 1977 I was already enrolled at the Finance Inspectors' School. These were the first years of the Monarchy, the beginning of democracy in Spain, after Franco's death. Ana passed her exams in April 1977 and we were married in October.

My First Political Steps

I was at the School until May 1978. Then came time for our first posting. Mine was to Logroño, so that's where we went. Back then, Logroño was a smaller, more intimate city. Ana had gotten a post as a civil government administration expert, and I was working for the local tax inspection office. We were both outsiders; we were a young couple. They had us pegged immediately.

The day after we arrived, we went to a very nice little restaurant where we'd been told they served great food. It was called Cachetero. A woman named Floren ran the place. As soon as we sat down, she came over and gave us the rundown of who we were: the young couple from Madrid, you're the tax inspector and you're in the civil government. She knew everything.

After I'd been working in the local office for a short while, people from different political parties started to come around. The UCD (Democratic Center Union) was very strong in Logroño. They had won three of the province's four seats in the 1977 elections. There were also people from Areilza's group, Liberal Citizens' Action, and people from Manuel Fraga's Democratic Coalition. And then the Popular Alliance started talking to me to see if I was interested in helping out.

At first, I wasn't very interested. But they said it would be really important for me to help get certain groups in Logroño to support the Constitution. In Logroño, as everywhere else, there were people who had qualms about the specifics in the constitutional text. I told them I was willing to lend a hand. And that's how I first got involved in politics, by setting up a Constitution meeting aimed at addressing the issues of people who were against it and gaining their support.

That meeting was where I met Fraga. And Fraga, of course, knew my father and my grandfather, Manuel Aznar. He had worked with both of them. So he lent me a hand, and continued to do so in the party, the Popular Alliance. One day they sent me to Madrid, to make contact with José María Areilza. I met him at the launch for his book That's How I Saw Them, a book of portraits. Areilza was an excellent writer, very fine, and it was great to see him and my grandfather together. Later Areilza called me and said he wanted me to let him negotiate with the Popular Alliance so that I could stand as the Democratic Coalition's number one candidate in Logroño. I said that, having just moved to Logroño my standing as number one on their electoral list was unthinkable. In the end, my friend Álvaro Lapuerta stood.

After meeting Fraga, I started working with the Popular Alliance in preparation for the 1979 election campaign. I did whatever needed to be done: picked people up when they needed rides to the meetings; made announcements over a megaphone to inform the public about party functions; put posters up, because back then you were still allowed to hang posters. That campaign was a total catastrophe. They'd made posters that had a brown background, with black and white photos of Fraga, and then the rest of the candidates underneath. You couldn't see anything, and what little you could see was terrible. The Democratic Coalition, the umbrella organization that combined the Popular Alliance and Areilza's group, took a real beating, as did some others.

But since I like a challenge, I decided not to quit. I didn't join the party, but I started to go by the headquarters, in Espolón Plaza, more regularly. Later I filled out my membership card, and when they invited me to the Popular Alliance provincial party conference in La Rioja, I knew it was time to make a decision to become more involved. They asked me to be provincial party secretary, and I agreed. Fraga had stepped down as leader of the Popular Alliance after the March 1979 elections, and at the time the party organization was based on provincial general secretaries. After Fraga returned at the end of 1979, the party adopted a presidential structure, which is what it still has.

That was when a commission to negotiate the La Rioja statute of autonomy was created. I took part in the meetings as a consultant for the Popular Alliance representatives, and since I had expertise in the area, given my job as tax inspector, I was able to literally take part in creating Spain's organization as a State of Autonomies.

Those were the two things I did at the start of my political career. Back then, a party like the Popular Alliance wasn't exactly brimming over with young people, and I spent my early days in it trying to persuade people who were uncomfortable with the country's new political situation to support the Constitution. Those who had their reservations had to be convinced that the Constitution was a step forward, something very positive for Spain.

The question of the Autonomous Communities also aroused suspicion in certain sectors of society. The socialists wanted La Rioja and Navarra to form part of the Basque Country. Others wanted La Rioja to be part of Castilla y León or part of Aragón. That wasn't a ridiculous proposition, like the first one, but in the end, the people chose what they wanted to choose, as we saw in the request for the autonomous process to be opened up, voted for by almost every La Rioja municipality. But it was the same as with the Constitution. You had to talk to people, convince them, explain the benefits of what was, back then, a project that still wasn't clearly defined.

Shortly thereafter, in the early 1980s, the first Basque parliamentary elections were held. We almost didn't stand, but a party activist insisted that we had to and managed to convince Fraga. They asked me to help out in Álava, one of La Rioja's provinces, so I went to every town in the province and handed out electoral propaganda, getting out the word about our party. There was one occasion I'll never forget. We were holding a meeting at a movie theater in Vitoria. The place was almost empty and the meeting was practically a secret. I was party representative for the elections. We got two seats.

I look back on those years fondly, nostalgically. We were very young, we had so much to do, we worked hard and we had a great time. My first son, José María, was born in Logroño. It's amazing to see how much both Logroño and La Rioja have changed since then. When I go back, I have mixed emotions. I am so happy that it's become such a rich, prosperous region. But I'm also glad that the people there haven't changed. They're still good, honest, hard-working people. I still have friends there.

Member of Parliament for Ávila in 1982

We returned to Madrid in 1980 at Christmastime. Then, between 1981 and 1982, they started to negotiate the Autonomous Agreements and they asked me to help. In 1981 I was named Party Vice-Secretary for the Autonomous Communities and in February 1982 I was elected at a general conference. These negotiations were prior to what would become LOAPA (the Organic Law for the Harmonization of the Autonomous Process). Present were Rodolfo Martín Villa, the Minister of Public Administration, and Manuel Broseta, the Secretary of State who was later assassinated by ETA. Shortly before he was murdered, in 1992, I talked to him about joining the Popular Party. Both men were standing for the UCD, as was Juan Manuel Reol de Tejada, who had been President of Pre-Autonomous Castilla y León. Santiago Carrillo, Enrique Curiel and Carlos Alonso Zaldívar were also there, standing for the Communist Party, and María Izquierdo and Alfonso Guerra for the Socialists. Álvaro Lapuerta and I were standing for the Popular Alliance. There I was, just in from La Rioja, 27 years old. It was the first time I set foot in 3 Castellana, which is where the Prime Minister's central office used to be. And in the daily meetings there, that is where I got to know all those people.

In the end, the UCD government and the PSOE – the Socialist Workers' Party – signed the agreements. It's not that we didn't want to sign them; but they sidelined us so they wouldn't have to share their role. Back then I still wasn't sure about my leap into professional politics. Ana still didn't like the idea; she hadn't liked it from the start. At the time there was no conflict of interest. I had my regular job in the morning, and I went to political meetings in the evening. Unpaid, of course.

But I really liked my political role. And deep down, I wasn't passionate about being Tax Inspector. I had passed my test join the civil service because I wanted to get married and have stability and I was very satisfied. The Treasury is an important part of the state. But when, soon after my arrival in Madrid, they sent me to the national headquarters where they manage all of the regional treasury offices, which is part of the Ministry of Finance, I was happy to go. I'd been working as an inspector in Logroño for two and a half years and in Madrid for six months. Besides, my professional work had a lot in common with my political work, because the national headquarters was where important devolution directives were being formulated.

That is where they decided how to calculate the effective cost of services that were going to be devolved; it's where they drew up tax laws and dealt with state revenue allocation. All the big finance laws relating to the Autonomies were fleshed out there. They negotiated with the Autonomies to apply the Organic Law of Autonomous Community Financing; they decided on the important transfers of power; they designed the Interregional Compensation Fund. And two other very important negotiations took place there: the Basque Country Economic Order and the draft. I worked as a state civil servant on the technical side, helping draft the autonomous finance laws and then again, when I was Prime Minister and the laws underwent important changes. So I was there, combining my professional career with my participation in the political sphere. And politics was becoming more and more attractive.

In 1982 Fraga asked me to stand as a Member of Parliament for the province of Soria. It was problematic because the party was very disorganized there. In fact, the party didn't want me there. And that was when Fraga called to offer me another province: Ávila. After what had happened in Soria I was somewhat discouraged, and I worried that the same thing would happen again. So I didn't want to take Fraga's call. Right then, my wife Ana made a decision. "If you want to be a Member of Parliament," she said, "this is your chance." I jumped in the car and drove to Ávila. Ávila was still Adolfo Suárez territory, even though by then the UCD had split and Suárez had founded his own group, the CDS (Social and Democratic Center). People thought that of the three seats, one would go to the UCD, one to the CDS, which was standing with Suárez's support, and one to the PSOE, the Socialist Party.

Well, that's what they thought. Those in the know made it clear to me that I had no chance. But regardless, I had to contend with the pace in Ávila, and to the fact that the party had no real base or structure there. One day they'd tell me to come in at one o'clock, and the next day at two. I could see that things were moving very slowly, but I couldn't say anything. I was an outsider and had no way to impose anything.

Then one morning, I was waiting for someone in a cafeteria, and Feliciano walked in. Feliciano Blázquez became a good friend, and he still is. He asked me if I thought I was going to win the elections by sitting in a cafeteria. Of course not, I said, but what can I do? He asked me if I was willing to go to El Barco, a town in Ávila where they were having a fair, the next day. And I knew immediately that he was my kind of guy. We got in the car and went. We got filthy from head to toe, but we hit the streets, house by house, town by town.

And we won the elections. In fact the Popular Alliance even got more votes than the CDS – with Agustín Rodríguez Sahagún heading the electoral list - and the Socialists. The UCD didn't win a single seat. And that's the story of how what would become the Popular Party was as important as the UCD once was. Or at least that's how the story begins.

The PSOE victory in 1982 was a landslide, but I was happy that night. We had won in Ávila, which was tough, and I was a Member of Parliament at 29. One day I'd have to sit down and reorganize my life, but for the time being I could still juggle having a seat in Parliament and being a civil servant. There was a group of young representatives in the house, people who'd just been elected to Parliament: Rodrigo Rato, Juan Ramón Calero, Arturo García Tizón and others. And since we were the youngest, we were in charge of parliamentary discipline. It wasn't easy, because it was a very heterogeneous group: there were the old hands, the relatively new people, and then the greenhorns, like us.

There were also people of every ilk and manner, some with strong personalities and hugely contrasting ways of thinking. There were people from the Popular Alliance, the Democratic Popular Party, folks from the Liberals Clubs, the Liberal Party, some regionalists like Hipólito Gómez de la Roces, and friends from the Navarra People's Union, like Jesús Aizpún.

That's where we started to flesh out the Statutes of Autonomy, the second phase of the Autonomic State. And since I was well versed in these matters, I started work on helping out with parliamentary tasks, taking part in commissions and acting as spokesperson. We formed what was called the Inter-Parliamentary Commission to coordinate the Members of Parliament from the different Autonomies.

Understanding what we were up against from the beginning was crucial. There was the Socialist Party, with some two hundred Members of Parliament; there were a few people from the UCD, almost lost in the tide; and then there was Adolfo Suárez at the top. And there we were huddled over in the right corner, with the assorted collection of people that made up the Popular Group. That wasn't right; it didn't add up. It didn't correspond to how I saw Spanish society.

Within the party there was something that we disagreed profoundly on, and that was the scope of the Socialists' electoral victory. Although now it seems absurd, there were people who thought that in essence their victory was a response to the UCD split and that soon things would be back to normal. That was a pretty common belief with party veterans. I disagreed entirely. I thought people had made their desire for change very clear, and as far as I was concerned it wasn't the kind of political change you see in secure democracies. This wasn't just standard power switching. It was a sea change of historic transcendence, and as such it had unleashed a movement that was destined to last a long time. Something beyond anyone's control might possibly derail it, but that was unlikely. We were facing a Socialist majority that was going to last a long time.

The center-right, in turn, was facing a paradoxical situation. The Popular Alliance had 106 Members of Parliament. In 1979 the party had almost become extinct. We went from having almost nothing (nine representatives in the previous term) to making up a considerable representative group. The municipal elections in 1979 had been catastrophic. But what mattered were the 1982 elections. In a very short space of time, between 1979 and 1982, we had made substantial progress. That said something about our base, who had stuck by us in tough times. And we started to see that the UCD had done their job and they now had to make way for another political force.

The transition was made possible thanks to Manuel Fraga, and now a real alternative was starting to take shape. I admire Fraga for his political career, for his hard work and intellectual curiosity, his tenacity and his faith in what he called "Project Spain". I owe him an awful lot, because he was generous enough to believe in me during some very important moments in my career. But more than all that, which is already very important, is the fact that in part he made me what I was, and what I still am. Fraga embodies the sort of deep personal generosity and moral and intellectual honor that has always served as a model for me.

In spite of all that, the Popular Group wasn't as strong or as fit as it needed to be. On one side was Fraga, with his own personality and a group of young people working on whatever they could and whatever they thought needed to be done; on the other was a group of barons, people with great influence who had had important roles in Spain's transition to democracy and wanted to maintain those roles. It was very clear to me that we needed to reposition ourselves, to move back to the center, to a space that the Socialists had made theirs.

And we had to try to reorganize the party in order to do so. We had to build a strong, solid party that would let us get back to the center. That was the goal.

A Party in Crisis

Once the party had begun to shift, Fraga asked me to be president of the Autonomous Community of Castilla y León. That was back in early 1983 and Castilla y León was in a huge mess, being pulled between Burgos on one side and León on the other. I was happy being a Member of Parliament, and Ana, my wife, didn't want to leave Madrid. I turned down Fraga's request, saying it was not the right time. He didn't speak to me for three months.

The 1983 autonomous elections proved to us that we had a serious organizational problem in Castilla y León. We couldn't even put forth just one candidate for the regional Presidency, because all of the people who headed the provincial lists considered themselves candidates.

The 1986 elections marked a low point in terms of recovering the party. The NATO referendum had thrown us. It was foolish, and my party's abstention was a mistake. I always thought we should be in NATO. In addition to that, though, Miquel Roca's Reform Operation got involved, supposedly with the aim of creating a center alternative in Catalonia. It was predictably unsuccessful, but it did stop us from gaining strength as a center party. The whole thing resulted in party stagnation. That, combined with the Popular Coalition defeat in the 1986 Basque elections – which in turn led to a coalition government between the Basque Nationalist Party and the Socialist Workers' Party – resulted in Fraga resigning as party leader in November of the same year. Part of the coalition left the day after the elections.

By then Fraga had asked me to run for President of Castilla y León again. In June 1985 I had become the regional party president. I accepted because it was a good career opportunity and also an opportunity to widen the party's geographic base. As part of our restructuring, I felt we also had to take on responsibilities in the Autonomies.

When Fraga resigned they convened a special legislature, in February of 1987. I was working in a group headed up by Miguel Herrero, who was the parliamentary spokesman. Rogrigo Rato, Federico Trillo, Loyola de Palacio and others were also there. Our aim was to give the people what they wanted, that is, a substantial change. Miguel Herrero was the most well known figure in the group and he represented continuity in Fraga's absence. Herrero would allow party renovation without rupture. In the lead was the list headed by Antonio Hernández Mancha, who had gotten good results in the 1986 autonomous elections in Andalusia. A good number of regional party organizations and some vice-presidents also supported him.

The closer we got to the assembly the more we realized that we were going to take a serious beating. We were headed straight for disaster, in fact. If we survived, it would be by sheer luck. Two days before the assembly I met with Herrero and said that we should really think hard about presenting his list because we were going to be defeated. He said he wasn't giving up regardless, and I said that in that case, neither was I. In fact, there were a lot of people and many friends who supported us. But in the end what we had foreseen did happen.

As if that weren't enough, in April 1987, Rodolfo Martín Villa from the PDP – the Democratic Popular Party – announced that he was going to stand for President of Castilla y León. That was quite a surprise, because I had been named a few months earlier at a meeting in Burgos that Fraga attended, and besides, I was regional party president. Martín Villa had been minister during the UCD period and he was quite a powerful rival, but I didn't even consider standing down, not for even a second. Why should I? I was convinced that we could win, as we had in Ávila in 1982. Given that those were such disconcerting times for the party, it was crucial that we build a wide geographic base. If we did, we could begin to think about a new position for the party. If not, then things were going to get rough.

Antonio Hernández Mancha, who had won the assembly, responded well. He said that if I wanted to continue with my candidacy then that was all there was to it.

President of Castilla y León

We won the 1987 elections, but we didn't get an absolute majority. We got 32 Members of Regional Parliament, and another one who supported us in the investiture. The Socialists got a few seats, too, and the CDS got 19, which was quite impressive. This was a critical moment. Our party, which had won 107 seats in the 1986 general elections, now had 67 because of the PDP and other Members of Parliament who went with them, under very poor counsel I might add. So, we were going through a crisis. And that was the precise moment when Antonio Hernández Mancha decided to lodge that censure motion against Felipe González.

Given the good turnout that the CDS had gotten in Castilla y León, I don't know what would have happened if Adolfo Suárez had had his political reflexes working properly. That's why it was vital for us to strengthen our hold in Castilla y León. We were already in power in Galicia, in the Balearic Islands and in Cantabria, although in less than exceptional circumstances. But Castilla y León would be the party's first large, centrally located region, the first one with a lot of municipalities. Getting into office there would be a little bit like starting to dream. And we had to try.

Because of our negotiations with the CDS we were governing alone at first. In spite of being a minority, it was hugely gratifying. We wanted to conquer the world, we had new initiatives every week; we were unstoppable. We were a very young group of great, brilliant, truly extraordinary people. That's where the teams that I continued to work with over the years were first formed. We had advisors, like Juan José Lucas and Jesús Posada, and people who drew up the initiatives aimed at renovating politics completely: Mercedes de la Merced, who, in addition to continuing to work in the party, was also City Councilor in Madrid for many years; Miguel Ángel Cortés, Secretary of Culture; Carlos Aragonés, who led my cabinet; Ana Mato, in charge of party organization; Miguel Ángel Rodríguez, Government Spokesperson; Juan Carlos Aparicio, Minister of Labor and now Mayor of Burgos, and many others.

It was amazing, to be in Castilla y León, the heart of the country, and be able to put our ideas into action, ideas based on liberalism that we had hashed out over the previous years. We immediately introduced measures to limit spending: we cut consultancies and high-level posts; we limited expense accounts and useless expenditure; we introduced austerity measures. Then we boosted industrial output; we created business parks; we tried to provide the region with ways to modernize; and we also began to recover and restore their historical and cultural heritage. That was unbelievably ambitious, because the scope and magnitude of Castilla y León's cultural and artistic heritage is astonishing.

Castilla y León is also where we started to enact liberalization policies and budgetary controls that we went on to fine-tune and then apply throughout Spain. For us, it was proof of hope for the future. And it was awesome.

Within a short time those measures became a show of what the party could do if we put our minds to it. Soon, people came to see us from all over the place, people from within the party but also union representatives and business leaders who wanted to see what we were doing. Valladolid became a place of pilgrimage, where people came to see what the new center-right could do from a position of power. So the idea of a pact with the CDS began to seem like a good way to lend us some stability. We talked about it more and more. I remember one conversation with Adolfo Suárez in his office, located on calle Antonio Maura in Madrid. It was a really agreeable, very open conversation. And he basically told me that he really liked the idea of us working together.

That's how the pact with the CDS came to be. First came a stable government in Castilla y León. Two CDS representatives joined the autonomous government, and we had their support in the Regional Parliament, which meant we were no longer a minority government. Then came the censure motion in Madrid's city council, so CDS got into power in Madrid and Agustín Rodríguez Sahagún – who had been a Regional Member of Parliament with me back in Ávila – became Mayor of Madrid.

But something else happened before that: the 1989 conference. Things were going well in Castilla y León, but not in the party. In fact, quite the opposite. Things were going downhill fast. Some irresponsible individuals wanted to destabilize the Castilla y León parliamentary group, and they were maneuvering against us. I realized that in a few short weeks we could lose everything we'd gained from our efforts. I didn't want to go against anyone - not then and not later – but I was not going to stand back and let everything we'd worked for be destroyed. So I spoke to Fraga. Fraga wanted to wait, to give things a chance to cool down. I told him that we couldn't, there was no time to waste.

That was all in preparation for the 1989 conference, which turned out well. Fraga became president of the party again. I was elected vice-president. That conference was where the new party was launched; that was when the old PDP, the Christian Democrats and the liberals all joined the Popular Party, as we were called from that moment on.

Marcelino Oreja had encouraged that union and he topped the Popular Party's lists in the European elections in June 1989. It had been a very successful conference but the message hadn't reached the public clearly. The European elections were a resounding failure. After the euphoria of the conference came dejection. Felipe González took advantage of that negative atmosphere by putting forward the general elections by eight months: they should have been held in June 1990, not October 1989. And after the European election failure, the polls predicted we would have catastrophic results in the general elections.

Everyone said it was going to be a disaster. We were going to lose half of the seats we'd gained with Fraga in 1986. If we were lucky, we'd end up with 80 Members of Parliament. That was what they were predicting anyway. Things were moving fast and I thought it was my responsibility to head our lists. So we had to pick up and move to Madrid immediately, with our three children, and had to move into a house that wasn't ours, because we had rented ours out. We stuck our furniture in storage. But it was all worth it. The PSOE got 175 seats, almost an absolute majority. It was a clear victory, yes, but it wasn't like 1982 when we saw a Socialist tide roll in. And we got 107 seats. Not only had we not lost, as everyone predicted. We had held our ground, and even advanced.

That really encouraged the party and it helped us win the autonomous elections in Galicia. That was the first time Fraga ran in Galicia, and it was clear that if he didn't win by an absolute majority he wasn't going to rule there. It was crucial for him to become President of the Galician autonomous government. Fraga was very open about it, and he said to me, "Never has anyone done so much in so little time."

Moving Towards the Center

The tenth party conference was held in April 1990, and I made the decision to disregard all of the party vice-presidents. There were eight of them, and it made decision-making nearly impossible and diluted responsibilities. You can't work like that. There has to be one person in charge, and that person is the president. Fraga told me that there had to be some acceptable middle ground, between eight and one. Two, for example. And I said it was all or nothing. It was impossible to carry on with the system we had with eight vice-presidents. Someone had to take responsibility. I was elected president of the party. At that point, I had already handed Fraga a letter of resignation, undated, and when he went before the conference, he ripped it up in front of everyone. That was a really spectacular gesture.

A few months earlier, on November 9, 1989, the Germans had

torn down the Berlin Wall. That victory presented a challenge for us. Real socialism had collapsed in the East. Now Spain had to present a viable alternative to the Socialist Party. There was no longer any socialist ideological hegemony as there had been in the Eighties. What had once been called the "social progress block" had crumbled because the Spanish social situation had changed, so there was a demand for a change in political power, too. We could no longer afford to be in it just to survive, as we had until then. We had to actually go out there and try to win, like the Germans had. The future of Spain was at risk, for several generations. We had to inspire a new style of politics; we had to promote a liberal society free of tutelage and state controls; we had to promote an efficient state. And in order to do so, we needed a different kind of Popular Party, one that would pull together and leave behind infighting.

We thought that in order to advance our project and actually land in government we'd need two terms, starting from 1990. It would take one term to bring the issues to the people, as the Socialist Party had many years before when they cleaned house, stopped living in a culture of exile and resistance and got in touch with reality. We had to build a party with a center platform and mindset, and we had to organize it in such a way that there would be no more ill defined factions and splinter groups. That meant that we had to open the way for new blood. The people who were already there had done a great job and they had fulfilled their mission. We had to be considerate, though. We had to find new leadership, reposition, and spell out a clear, solid platform.

There had been very important people present at that Seville party conference, people like Mariano Rajoy, Rodrigo Rato, Federico Trillo and Francisco Álvarez Cascos. We were facing the challenge of building a strong party, a great party with a platform that would gain the confidence of an electorate who had watched what happened to the Spanish center-right in bewilderment. Francisco Álvarez Cascos, who was confirmed as Popular Party General Secretary, turned out to be a key figure in shaping the new project. He commanded unquestionable authority from the start.

The party really had to show that it was moving to the center; we had to show that we were moderates, that we were the party for people who don't want to be told what to do and who prefer to take responsibility for their own lives and their own decisions. Just as we didn't want anyone to our right, we also didn't want anyone else between the PSOE and us. We had to fill that space. That meant we had to include, not exclude. The whole range of centers had to be included in the Popular Party, keeping in mind the premise that there was no longer any room for factions. There were no Christian Democrats, no liberals, no little subgroups. We were all one.

We needed the UCD to join the Popular Party, and they did. But we still had to get the CDS. Why? Because I had claimed the legacy and the legitimacy of the UCD, the organization that had undertaken the country's transition to democracy after Franco's death. The CDS, who had sprung directly from the UCD, was resisting. That was an obstacle that kept us from growing and decreased voter confidence, because they could see that there were two parties with very similar ideologies and political aspirations. Eventually, though, they joined us. And Adolfo Suárez joked that it was because of me that he retired early from politics.

Getting the CDS and UCD to join us was the first step. Then we had to go even further. Not only did we have to position ourselves adjacent to the PSOE, we also had to actually win over some of the Socialist Party's voters. We had to offer alternatives, promote a new ideology, open doors and throw off the yoke that had been holding us back: the idea that we were a party of the past. We couldn't keep allowing that kind of discrimination, which is based on a prejudice against the entire history of Spain.

FAES (the Social Issues and Analysis Foundation) played an important role in our repositioning. You need clear ideas and projects to engage in politics, and if we wanted to get into to power in Spain we had to debate seriously and realistically, we had to challenge people's ways of thinking, debate the ethics and determine the decisions that are made, and the boundaries between public and private. With FAES we were able to rethink our actions, our aims and our platform. They also helped by getting people who did not share our way of thinking to collaborate. Anyone who had something interesting to say was welcome, regardless of ideology. I went to the meetings, took part in the debates, and collaborated wherever I could. That was the intellectual and generational expression of what we wanted to achieve. We were very discrete, we didn't ask for any public commitments. FAES are not image-makers; that's not what it was about. It was about building a platform and giving the Spanish center-right its own sphere, its rightful position, and it was about regaining the center in terms of ideas, too.

FAES was a liberal organization, in step with my education and my current way of thinking. It's true that I was never a Christian Democrat. For historical reasons, the Christian Democrats never really took shape in Spain. But just because FAES was liberal didn't mean that we were excluding anyone from the project. I never made people define themselves ideologically, one way or the other. I've always respected any ideology that is fundamentally based on the principle of responsibility. So from the very beginning dialogue and respect were at the heart of our way of doing things. It was natural for other parties to join us, and they did, freely. And we all agree on the fundamental principles of freedom, stability and reform.

You can't disregard the contribution Christian Democracy made to the reconstruction of a number of European countries, or their role in building the European Union, which is evident in the current European Popular Party. The European Popular Party is not just a conglomeration of national parties; it's a wholly European organization based on common values, with policies aimed at achieving prosperity and stability. It is a party that is now attempting to draw up a center reformist proposal for all the countries in the Union. And it's also a forum for debate and communication that we in the Spanish Popular Party have contributed to. This forum has been tremendously useful for dealing with issues and questions that, previously, had remained entirely in the domestic realm. If you truly believe, as I do, that stable democracies require strong parties, then a vote for the European Popular Party is a vote for the future.

But getting back to our situation in the early Nineties, it was very important for us not to repeat the coalition model, which was traditional in the Spanish center-right. Leadership had to be exclusive and the leader had to be the one making important decisions, since he would have to answer for them. But in order to build up the organization you also have to delegate. I am very much in favor of delegating responsibilities. But if you delegate them, you also have to make sure that they're fulfilled, that people follow through. So just as I made it clear that I wasn't going to repeat the vice-presidential system where nobody has ultimate responsibility for making decisions, I also made it clear that I had no interest in secret meetings, social gatherings and restaurant get-togethers in Madrid. That scene didn't interest me back then and it doesn't interest me now. We had to build an unstoppable party with members who were held accountable and leadership that was indisputable. We had to be a party to reckon with. And we had to do it without leaving anyone out, yet keeping a clear picture of what we wanted. I didn't want to sideline anybody. Those who left did so because they weren't interested in the project, or because they were interested in pursuing other things, or because they thought we were going to fail.

At the same time as all of this was going on – in 1989 – the Popular Party joined the European Popular Party and started working internationally with parties like ours. At first, because of the transitional periods required, we were just observers, and then we became full members. They were a little bit suspicious of us. The PSOE had been in power for eight years and there wasn't much short-term hope of that changing. In addition, in just a few short years we had presented some candidates who differed from each other remarkably. They must have thought we weren't particularly dependable. But I knew that this was for real. And our international position took shape. And then we ended up joining the International Christian Democrats, who changed their name to the International Center Democrats; I am currently their president.

1990-1996: The Opposition Years

Life has a pace of its own, and it doesn't necessarily correspond to our predictions. We had predicted that we'd need one term, from 1989 to 1994, to reposition, reorganize and get through to the public. Then in the second term, from 1994, we'd have four more years to advance politically so that in 1998 we could get into office. That was our strategy.

In 1990 we started to see the light, after one of the party's most critical moments, when we almost fell off the map. Three years later, in 1993, we were forced to stand in the elections that we'd thought were going to be the ones where we got our position through to the electorate, where we'd continue to occupy the center space. Things went much differently than we'd planned, however. We had to go for it.

This requires some explanation. In the first place, in 1989 the PSOE had won by a very close margin. They no longer had the overwhelming majority that they'd had enjoyed up until then. Then, after the December 1989 general strike, they started entering into agreements with trade unions and shot public spending up dramatically; this led to economic measures that started a serious economic crisis.

The Barcelona Olympics and the World Expo in Seville served as distractions, although there's no doubt that these were two very important events. But beneath that shiny exterior lurked reality: the country was in a terrible depression. People talk about the 1993 crisis but the truth of the matter is that things really started to go downhill in 1992, even though it didn't seem like it at the time. The international crisis had already begun, and Spain was hit even harder because the Socialist government took the wrong economic measures. The huge celebrations in

1992 covered up what was really happening, but that is when massive job losses began; by the end of 1993 our unemployment rate had reached 23% and the public deficit was over 7% of the GDP. All that began in 1992; Spanish society changed a lot that year.

If we were really going to try to get into office we couldn't ignore the facts. That reality meant that, in spite of everything we had planned – the period of internal organization, bringing our ideas to the public, maturation – we had to really go out in the 1993 campaign and try to get elected. That was the first year I really took part in the elections, the first time I was intensely involved. In 1989 we'd done everything in a rush. We'd only had a month and a half to get ready and frankly it was a miracle that I'd managed to save the furniture. But in 1993 it was different; I had time to undertake a serious campaign, one that was politically focused on what a party's goal should really be.

And in fact, the Popular Party gained a significant increase in those elections. We shot up from 5,286,000 votes in 1989 to 8,201,000 in 1993. That's an increase of almost three million voters, and from then on we've done better and better in every general election. A lot of people thought we might win, they were expecting victory. The Socialists were so worried that they had to agree to something they had never before agreed to: televised debates. They were convinced that the debates would work in their favor.

Well, my first debate with Felipe González dashed those hopes. The Popular Party showed itself for what it was: a serious alternative. There was certainly no problem measuring up to the PSOE leaders. That fateful feeling pervading political life, that gnawing sensation that there was no way to beat the Socialists, was suddenly dispelled. And that's when they resorted to every trick in the book to keep the responsibility of running the government from falling to us. They formed an enormous coalition to impede a Popular Party victory. They used the campaign to scare people and they lied about what we would do if elected.

I had already overcome a lot of obstacles and a lot of attempts at destabilization; they tended to come from outside the party, from certain sectors of business, the media and other hangers-on who like to move in circles of power. In any case, they fell back on a tactic that the Socialists use quite frequently: character assassination. I had quite naturally used the first debate to explain my platform, and they decided to pulverize me. I'm not talking about a discussion of ideas, or your platform, or even leadership potential. They go for the jugular, they really try to destroy you. To make you out to be a caricature, to sneer at your beliefs, to make out that what you think is some historical aberration. It's one of the things Spanish Socialist leaders and those around them excel at; that's just the way they are.

All that on top of the historic prejudice that weighs against the center-right in Spain, and against Spanish history in general. The way they see it, if you're not on the left, you're ultra-right. And therefore, naturally, in no fit state to think, write, teach, and certainly you can't be allowed to rule. These prejudices have devastating effects. But we overcame them this time. We have never, ever sunk so low as to use that type of attack. And if you refrain from making the same mistake, from dirty campaigns, you forge your character. If you're attacked on a personal level and you don't retaliate, you come out ahead for it.

As I said, I've never been concerned with image. I've never paid much attention to that kind of thing. A certain European politician, a neighbor of ours, had a moustache and they told him to shave it off for the elections and he did. They said the same thing to me. They said that if I shaved off my moustache, I'd be guaranteed at least a five-point increase. It was hilarious.

I've never had any special parliamentary training, either. I've been a Member of Parliament for many years, I've worked on a lot of commissions and been up and down the platform more times than I can count. I've taken part in all sorts of debates, from the VAT Law to the Local Rule, from investiture debates to the State of the Nation debates, both in opposition and in government. If you're going to be a parliamentarian you have to be on commissions and take part in debates. And if you want to get into office you have to cut your teeth in all of them, even if they seem dry. Budget debates, for example, are important because they give you a chance to articulate intelligible discourse on economic policy, which is the key to a government's politics.

I always liked being active in Parliament. You have to be geared up mentally for debates, have to have good reflexes to respond to objections, and you have to have your material planned, have to know what you want to say. That's what really counts. The rest is just for show.

The meeting in Mestalla Stadium, in Valencia, during the 1996 campaign, was the most spectacular I've taken part in and probably the most spectacular in the history of Spanish democracy. This one was particularly exciting. Although I've always enjoyed meetings in Valencia, I tend to prefer them in different types of venues, especially the bullring. I like political meetings where I can communicate with people, see who's attending, talk to everyone. The Mestalla gathering was so huge that it was impossible to make contact with the people at the back. In a bullring, there is a certain intimacy. Plus, Valencia is such a lively, vibrant city. I always feel at home with Valencians, and that's obvious at the meetings.

From the start I was convinced that we would win the general elections once we managed to turn around the situation in Madrid and Valencia. That's why I always paid such close attention to those two regions.

Although we didn't end up winning, in retrospect I'm sure that the Spanish people were right to not elect us that time around. Voters were effectively telling us that we were doing a good job, but that they wanted proof we could keep making progress. I'm not going to go out and say that I'm actually happy we lost in 1993. But I can say that in 1996 I was totally convinced that we had matured and were ready for office, and in 1993 I'm not so sure we were.

The problem was that though we might not have matured to the extent we needed to, the Socialists had gone way over the line. To put it differently, the Socialists had betrayed the public's faith. In spite of the fact that the Catalan nationalists backed them, their 1993 to 1996 term was a foregone conclusion. In essence, they proved our theory that they were out of touch with Spanish society and with the changes that had occurred during their time in office.

During that time, we never resorted to the type of personal attacks that the Socialists have since employed against us. There were two crucial things between 1993 and 1996 that had nothing to do with us. One was corruption, which is something it seems the Socialists have still not shaken off, though at the time they tried to imply that what had occurred were isolated events. They weren't. The dirty campaign contributions exemplified by the Filesa front company were not an isolated case, just as the whole reserved funds scandal was not an isolated event. They were symptomatic of a mindset, an entire way of viewing the state. And we had absolutely nothing to do with it. We also had nothing to do with the denunciation of the anti-ETA Anti-Terrorist Liberation Group, which then resurfaced due to a legal judgment. We called for a Senate investigation committee; that's it.

Nevertheless, we obviously couldn't just sit back and refrain from fulfilling our duty, which was to demand political consequences for what had occurred and was already at the heart of public debate. What were we supposed to do, keep our mouths shut? I didn't enjoy making high power speeches in Parliament. Impassioned rhetoric and a bad temper are not my style. What I enjoyed in Parliament was being able to set out our plans. But I had an obligation then. There was no option; we couldn't choose a different kind of opposition, because what we were dealing with was not politics but the total and utter disintegration of political power.

The 1996 Electoral Victory

That was one of the reasons we won in 1996. The months before the election we knew that we had an almost astronomical advantage. And that hurt us. Not because Popular Party voters stayed home. In fact, we obtained huge increases: from 1,600,000 votes to 9,700,000 votes.

What hurt us was the incredible mobilization of voters faced with the imminence of a Popular Party victory.

That's when alarm bells really started to sound. The 1993 campaign was tough, and so was 2000. But 1996 was a whole lot tougher. Of all the electoral campaigns I've lived through, this was by far the most brutal. I remember it very well, because while I was speaking at meetings and waiting to go on live television, I could also see what they were broadcasting before and after my speeches. So while I'd talk about democratic regeneration, they'd put on ads about Francisco "the Doberman" Álvarez Cascos, or showing the Civil War, even going as far as showing Franco's Battle of the Ebro. They carted out every image they could possibly think of to stir up Spaniards' against us, to call to mind the darkest turbid moments of Spanish history trying to associate them with us somehow. In the long run, it may have backfired, because once all your dirty tricks have been played, there's nothing left to stir up and nothing compares to how brutal they were. I've never seen such an expression of rancor.

But what seemed like a clear victory ended up being quite a close one. A small victory, but when all is said and done, a victory nonetheless. Some people have tried to attribute the tight margin to the fact that we kept a low profile, that our campaign was moderate. I think just the opposite is true. If, rather than behaving like a government party, we had wasted our time lowering ourselves and responding to the ridiculous accusations our adversaries made against us, we probably would have lost again.

Despite of our efforts, the 1996 campaign was not the kind of campaign worthy of a solid democracy. What's more, the PSOE yet again had incredible political, financial and media backing. The people who supported the PSOE probably believed that what happened between 1992 and 1996 was exceptional and that they could just get past it and move on. They were wrong. Most of the Spanish population had realized that the Popular Party was a real government party. And they were sick and tired of the spectacle that the Socialist government was making of itself.

I can't say I was happy with the results. But I wasn't disappoint-ed either. I had already had the experience of winning the Castilla y León elections by 3,500 votes. So winning the general election by more than 300,000 didn't seem so bad, really. It almost seemed like the way it had to be. And besides, even though things have gone pret-ty well for me in life, it's also true that everything I've ever achieved has been achieved by virtue of sheer hard work.

The Spanish people sent us a message. They were saying, "We're sick of the Socialists and we want you in office. But be careful. Don't take it for granted. We want to see what you can do." It wasn't really a bad position to be in. I had no doubt that the Popular Party would lead and I also knew what I had to do. Of course from that second on, all sorts of manipulations aimed at keeping us out of power were launched.

First they tried for a caretaker government. That was absurd, because the Socialists had ruled as a minority since 1993. That attempt was grounded in the belief of the left's supposed moral superiority, which made them the only legitimate governing power. Then they relented and said that the Popular Party could rule, but not with Aznar as leader. That was the first time I had the "Maura, no" experience, which goes back to the personal opposition campaign against Antonio Maura at the turn of the century. Yet again, the party was equal to the task at hand and the dirty tricks didn't work. We formed a coalition government with the support of the Catalan Convergència i Unió and the Canary Island Coalition.

You have to be willing to overlook a lot of things in life, especially in politics. But I think it's important to remember that in 1996 some people tried to stop our democratically elected govern-ment from coming to power. I have been very careful to not let that experience affect my later actions. But I think that, in order to make sure it never happens again, we have to make sure that that is one thing we never forget.

CHAPTER THREE

The Legacy of Spain's Transition to Democracy

In 1983, shortly after the PSOE got into office, backed by over ten million voters, our party put out a pamphlet called "This can be fixed." It was a well-intentioned and optimistic explanation of what had happened, but it was totally out of touch with reality. What had happened in 1982 was not simply a change in leadership; it wasn't the sort of swing of the political pendulum you get in stable democracies. It was a sea change that demanded a new response from our party. It called for much more than a "fix."

Something similar happened to the Socialists in 1996. They didn't fully understand what had happened, and in fact, they still haven't managed to figure it out. But as long as they don't sit down and analyze the changes, as long as they're unable to face up to reality the way we did after 1982, they're going to have a difficult time getting back into office in Spain.

The change came in 1996 when the PSOE lost the elections. But only when the Popular Party won an absolute majority in 2000 was the country's historical normalization finally complete. Of course, there are still problems to be solved. There are regional nationalist movements and there are problems that became obvious in the opposition to the Iraq war. But in historical terms, the transition ended there, in 2000. The narrow margin of our victory in 1996 made it possible to believe that we were just a parenthesis in Spanish history. The 2000 election results made it clear that that was not the case, and showed that indeed there was a democratic center-right capable of ruling with the voters' support. The 2000 elections ended the rupture that the Spanish Civil War had begun.

The transition to democracy certainly did mark some milestones and their significance must not be undervalued. The 1978 Constitution was the main one; it was a meeting point for all political forces. It's the only Spanish constitutional text that was ever agreed on by every political party, the only one where no group imposed its interests on others. Before spelling out the text, two enormously important processes occurred. The first was what led to the UCD Constitution, which allowed for the promotion of change from reformist sectors from within and brought on board others who had reached the same conclusions from the outside. The second process was the one that led the Socialists to modernize their ideology and to abandon their radical edge. In the end, it's also what got them into power in 1982. The 1982 elections were another milestone in the history of the transition to democracy, when the left managed to convince voters that they were a credible alternative, truly capable of governing.

I was young at the time. I met the key players involved in the transition much later. My small contribution back then was simply to realize, as the general public did, that we couldn't go back to a political monopoly of power, that a new day had dawned. We were lucky to have leaders who were willing to ensure that the new era was not born of confrontation. Specifically, I'm talking about His Majesty King Juan Carlos, who led the whole process, but I'm also referring to other politicians and rulers. All of them, each with their own political leanings, respected that will. The more extreme of them had to make a greater effort, but they did, and the most important thing is that they quickly found a way to lay the groundwork for Spain's normalization.

I've always had a great relationship with Adolfo Suárez. If the Crown guaranteed continuity, Adolfo Suárez guaranteed the political stability that led to a stable democracy. He did an absolutely extraordinary job and we are all indebted to him for his achievements. Whenever I refer to center parties, I never forget Adolfo Suárez's example and his ability to unite and include. By the same token, it was logical for his political role to end where it did, after he had accomplished the enormous feat of getting the transition on track. There is no reason, however, for his role to have ended the *way* it did; that should never have happened. Suárez deserved a better finale than that.

Leopoldo Calvo Sotelo was a brave man. He took charge of the UCD at a very difficult time and took some important decisions, such as Spain's entry into NATO. If that decision had been respected, as it should have been and as it eventually was, we would have saved a lot of time and a lot of unnecessary nuisance. Adolfo Suárez has always been sympathetic to our aims in the Popular Party and what we've done in Parliament, and Leopoldo Calvo Sotelo has been willing to help out whenever necessary. They are two great men with a strong sense of duty and a strong sense of what they owe their country.

The Spanish transition to democracy has served as a model not just for Latin American countries, but also for European countries that democratized later. That is extraordinary political capital for Spain, in terms of prestige and influence. But in addition to the transition itself, our success as a country can now be seen as exemplary, too. We are proof that a peaceful transition to democracy is possible, and that the country that comes out of that transition can – if it puts its mind to it – become successful, prosperous and influential. That's a double example and a double legacy. It demonstrates, first, the will to see eye to eye and establish a model of respect, tolerance and cooperation; and second, the will to safeguard those achievements.

All politicians, regardless of our agendas, should make the effort to respect that legacy and, instead of questioning it, we should be inspired by it. All of the key players in the transition made the effort to fulfill their duty, which was to build a democratic system without falling into the temptation of splitting off. That was the mandate that the Spanish public had given them. And they proved that they were up to the task.

It was a truly remarkable effort. One era came to a close and another began, with no violence and no public confrontation. It was a question of putting an end to years of intransigence. Now you hear people on the left try to reassess the transition, question its validity, I guess in an attempt to question the legitimacy of the process that brought us to where were are now. That's absurd. The transition is one of the historical moments when we, as Spaniards, were definitively able to carry out what was being demanded of us. Anyone who wants to criticize that should test the waters before jumping in. Critics have to be sure of their arguments and careful of what they say. If you try to deny the transition's legitimacy then you also deny the legitimacy of the fourteen years of Socialist government that followed it, and the legitimacy of all those on the left – and not just on the right or in the center – who took part in the accords so generously and in such good faith.

At times it seems like some Spaniards get bored of stability. Look at the Restoration of the Monarchy, at the turn of the 20th century. Some people seemed to feel it wasn't worth defending twenty-five or thirty years of a liberal Constitution. Now, it seems some people are bored after twenty-five years of parliamentary monarchy. Well, I'm not. I'd like our democracy to become as traditional and longstanding as that of some northern European countries. Over two hundred years of democratic, constitutional continuity. That's worth dreaming about.

Unfortunately, that hasn't been the case in Spanish history. There have been too many splits, too much instability. Democracy takes time, because you have to internalize certain behaviors like respect and tolerance, and that's not something that happens by itself overnight. In fact, it doesn't happen by itself at all. It has to become a habit, a practice, a way of being. It takes years, but that's what we need. We need to achieve democratic normality and not get bored, even if it isn't dramatic and violent and exciting. A lack of constancy is one of our shortcomings. We get tired of things too quickly and for no reason.

We have to get used to functioning institutions, terms of office being completed, laws being followed, and taking turns in office being the natural result of popular elections and not of tumultuous historical events. We have to be strong enough not to fall into the childish temptation of smashing things because we're tired of them. That's why safeguarding the transition's legacy is so important. Because it will take a long time and profound changes in order to bring the long historical periods of instability that Spain has gone through to a close.

Everyone who was part of the transition made an effort to support those changes, and the center-right made particularly important contributions by committing to institutional change. The party negotiated vital social agreements and showed extraordinary generosity towards culture, an area where the center-right has never sought to exact revenge or impose exclusivity. It also laid the groundwork for what is now Spain's international position. Undeniably, each group made its own worthwhile contributions.

Perhaps what we're seeing now is that the psychological reshuffle the transition to democracy required is finally bearing fruit. Previously, one of the essentials of that change had been based on the left's supposed moral and historical superiority. In this view, only the left had the ideas and the values that would allow them to be a vehicle for change. Since they'd never governed, people could expect and hope for anything from them. Democratic change could not be founded on the right - the theory went - because that was a step backwards, into the past.

These days, reality has forced people to reevaluate those misconceptions. After a PSOE government from 1982 to 1996, it's no longer possible to say that the left bears none of the blame for all the problems afflicting society. Particularly not the ones created by the policies they themselves put in place. In 1989 the Berlin Wall fell, bringing down with it the notion of revolutionary change. Today the left spends its time doing exactly what they accused the right of doing during and following the transition. That's a mistake. The left can't keep harkening back to the past, and what's more to an imaginary past. And they can't keep maintaining the same positions they did before they had ever been in office. What the left really needs to do is dare to confront reality rather than just stirring up the past, digging up graves and exhuming bodies.

That won't get them anywhere. History can't be rewritten. You can interpret events differently, but you can't change what happened. You can't just keep saying that the Second Republic didn't work but it should have, and that as a result of the Civil War there should have been a truth and reconciliation process even though no one knows how that might have turned out. It's as if the Italians just sat around saying they should have supported the Allies in 1943 or the Americans kept arguing that they should have intervened in the Second World War before Pearl Harbor rather than after. Fine. So? Every country has its own historical process and needs to be able to mark the boundaries between the past and the present.

By constantly reevaluating the past, pretending that the present has been jeopardized by a past that never actually existed, they're really keeping alive a very old idea that claims that Spain is an exception, a country where things should be allowed to occur, which don't happen in other countries. They maintain that we have a debt to the past that no one else has; so we – as Spaniards – are forced to live in an illusory world that everyone else has long since left behind. Some people think we should keep being the exception: the country that used to be a destination for romantic travelers in search of the exotic and now the last stronghold of leftist resistance, the place where the Socialists, who lost it all in 1989, come to have a good time.

That's not the kind of reputation I want my country to have, frankly. I don't want to be anybody's exception. My country's past is as dignified as anyone else's and my duty as a Spaniard is to help make my country prosperous and free. I want to work to make Spain's democracy strong and lasting. That's what I care about.

That's what King Juan Carlos brought to bear during the transition. The Crown guaranteed the continuity of the historical process, and with its support, the transition could be undertaken free of upset. That's why the transition never could have happened without the Crown. It was also crucial for the other players involved, because they knew the Crown provided the much-needed framework for their agreements. At one time or another, all parties have to explicitly declare their loyalty to the Crown, and in doing so they accept a certain historical tradition. Shortly before the 25th anniversary of the Constitution, the King was able to gather all of the presidents of the Autonomous Communities: that shows the importance of the Monarchy.

The King again proved himself as guarantor of freedoms on February 23, 1981, when there was an attempted coup. That night, and the days that followed, the King showed that he had a role as the heir to a tradition and as the nation's representative. That's why in Spain everyone who wants to live in peace and freedom identifies with the King and sees that he represents our common, living history.

The King facilitates things. He knows exactly why he's there and what his role is. He fulfills his duty and shows dedication, discretion and competence. He is always willing to work in partnership with institutions and has always helped the constitutional apparatus work effectively. He is a model for us all.

So is the Queen. I am impressed by her deep sense of duty, her humanity, and her ability to reach out and touch the hearts of people while always fulfilling her role as Queen of Spain. Fortunately, we have an heir to the throne, the Prince of Asturias, who guarantees the Crown's continuity.

The History of a Great Country

I've tried to recover the Spanish liberal tradition and on more than one occasion I have made a personal effort to bring that tradition to light, to bring it out of the darkness where it lay due to historical rupture and confrontation. A center party like ours had to reclaim the liberal, or liberal-conservative, tradition; it's *our* tradition. We're not coming out of obscurity, nor out of some idea someone had in the Seventies. We're coming from a solid tradition that in spite of all the difficulties has never been broken. From Jovellanos back during the Enlightenment to those who, in good faith, are now trying to help build a modern, liberal state that guarantees individual rights, the lines of continuity run deep. That's what makes our intellectual tradition so great. Manuel Fraga has helped preserve those lines with his studies of conservative Spanish thought. I felt it was my duty to rescue them and bring them to light.

I am completely convinced that Spain is one of the great nations of Europe and of the world. Like all great nations, it has great responsibilities and an important leadership role. We have had some brilliant moments in our history and some questionable times, too. But we can't move our current discussions backwards, into the past. For example, it was absurd to argue about whether or not we should celebrate the anniversary of the Discovery of America just because we don't like some of the consequences the Discovery had. And it's absurd that we can't talk honestly about the Catholic Monarchs, Isabella and Ferdinand, who after all gave the country its political shape, without those debates becoming problematic. The same is true of the Restoration – the reign of Alphonse XII and María Cristina. For years we saw only negative, critical portrayals of that period, when in fact it was a time characterized by institutional stability, peaceful coexistence and a respect for freedom.

We had to reclaim the Spanish liberal tradition because it's part of Spanish history, it demonstrates our continuity, and allows us to examine our past serenely. Spaniards have to start looking at the past without an inferiority complex, because our history gives us more to be proud of than it does to be ashamed of. Spain is a great nation because it decided to take on tremendous responsibility for centuries. When it stopped, that's when our crisis of self-image set in. That's when we started to see ourselves as exotic, different from the rest of Europe, split off from Western countries, with nothing in common.

It was ridiculous. Spaniards have formed part of the whole Western enterprise and made fundamental contributions. We were never separate. We can be proud of our history. Recovering Spain's past is part of regaining a patriotic feeling, a national feeling that people said Spaniards no longer had, though personally I never believed it.

The leader of the Second Republic, Manuel Azaña, said that it was natural for him to feel Spanish. That's a good way of putting it. We can each have different ways of conceiving of our country, we can be more or less critical of different aspects of our tradition or identify to a greater or lesser extent with different events in our past. But we are all, naturally and historically, Spanish and we should express ourselves as Spaniards. I don't see why that's problematic.

Liberals and Conservatives

Azaña was a bad leader and a problematic writer, but he did have a very clear idea of the nation. As far as he was concerned, the country was above political regimes. He thought he could practice a national brand of politics not because there was only one way of going about politics that could be called national, but because all politics need to have the country's best interest at heart. Azaña felt that politics had to encourage national loyalty and even national pride, pride in being Spanish. That's why I always liked Azaña, ever since I started reading him when I was young.

I think Azaña forms part of the Spanish liberal tradition. That tradition was there already, but it had to be modernized, highlighted, brought to light. We had to make people see how important its role had been, but we had to do so honorably and also to criticize it when necessary. There are two figures I see as particularly critical within that tradition: Antonio Cánovas and Antonio Maura. Cánovas and Maura represent two milestones in the history of Spanish liberalism. Conservative liberalism, yes, but liberalism, nonetheless. Cánovas came out of a national crisis that culminated in the First Republic, in the 19th century. With this difficult crisis behind him, he was able to execute a historic national project: continuing the history of Spain, as he put it, and giving the country a liberal regime that respected freedoms and had strong, national institutions. Cánovas proved that

Spain's history could lead to a liberal conception of the country and its politics.

Maura was a more modern figure, a 20th century figure. Maura had certain things very clear, and he understood the need to democratize the regime he'd inherited from Cánovas and Sagasta. He wanted a smooth transition between a liberal, 19th-century regime like the Restoration and a democratic, parlimentary monarchy, which is what the 20th century called for. If he had managed it, we might have avoided a good part of the civil conflicts we saw in the 20th century. That's what Fraga undertook, though in different terms, because he had to deal with a different set of circumstances. Then a new generation took up the task, and our aim was to make the historical tradition compatible with democracy.

As far as I'm concerned there is no clear distinction between liberalism and conservatism. When I talk about Cánovas and Maura, to me they're both part of the Spanish liberal tradition, as are Sagasta and Canalejas, two other great figures from this lengthy tradition full of important figures. They were conservatives, but liberals nonetheless. The similarities between liberal and conservative thought can be seen very easily by the defeat of Marxism and the ideologies derived from it, which are deeply anti-liberal. When the Berlin Wall came down, economic efficiency triumphed; there is no doubt about that. But that efficiency is based on a series of values and principles: individual freedom, responsibility, human rights and respect for the law.

To continue Spanish history, Azaña's democratic patriotism cannot exist – and in fact could not exist – without a respect for the values behind the moral demands that Ortega's conservative liberalism represented.

Hayek made this very clear at the beginning of *The Constitution of Liberty*. Freedom is not a single value but rather the source and pre-existing condition needed for most moral values. I might imagine a situation of total freedom for myself, but that individual freedom would offer me far fewer opportunities than a free society would. A free society is a society that makes it possible to discover and take advantage of opportunities that would have been unimaginable without it.

It does this because it makes cooperation possible, and that, in turn, requires respect for others; that is, it requires the application of the principles that make up what Raymond Aron calls a "pluralist society," which is a society that respects the law and also respects a sense of obligation, which entails recognizing the legitimacy of the other person's arguments and the possibility of reaching an agreement that is satisfactory to both parties.

Some aspects of liberalism, no doubt, are open to criticism. Ortega sums them up well when he says that freedom makes us more demanding of ourselves, forces us, in exercising it, to examine our own concept of truth. There is always a risk of confusing freedom with relativism - what I called nihilism earlier - which is that state in which everything is seen as unfounded and impossible to prove. Personal freedom and autonomy, though, must be compatible with respect for institutions, and even for traditions and beliefs. It's vital that the principle of individual freedom never undermine stability, because for free societies that would be suicide. Tolerance, one of the basic principles of interpersonal relations, must not lead to the abdication of convictions. Self-interest, which is what society's prosperity rests upon, must not lead to individual selfishness, which is incompatible with the principles of solidarity and unity essential for maintaining democratic order.

Tony Blair often says that the tragedy of the 20th century British left is that it split from its liberal roots. That's true all over the world. Even in the US, in the Seventies, the Democrats yielded to the temptation of radicalism. Clinton, on the other hand, came to power on a more centrist platform, and things went well for him. His eight years in office saw extraordinary economic prosperity. But he also did well politically. Clinton, like Blair, should be seen as a model for the new left, a left that would have understood what was behind the fall of the Berlin Wall, which was far more than economic freedom.

Blair's problems with the Labour left in the UK and the

rediscovery of the Democrats' radical tradition in the US stemming from opposition to the Iraq War prove that it's easier to combine liberalism with conservatism than it is to combine liberalism with leftist politics. There's no doubt about that. We don't need to exclude anyone from our project or our ideology. We need to apply our ideas and our principles.

Opposition and the Limits of Consensus

The way I see it, it would be absurd to complain that the opposition is not in good shape. But I will say that I miss having a figure like Sagasta. I would have liked someone with historical vision as opposition speaker, someone with a national and global perspective on problems. We made an effort when we were in opposition. We signed the Autonomous Agreements in 1992, the Toledo Pact in 1995, and whenever Spain's position in the world was at stake, we kept on in the same vein. That's what we did during the Gulf War in 1991, and in the Bosnian intervention in 1993, when Spain sent almost 1,500 soldiers.

On other occasions we tried to get the government to make wiser decisions by offering our own, corresponding proposals. They were always serious, never destructive proposals. On those matters, it was important for each party to be clear on its role, and for that to prevail.

One problem is that I've had so many different opposition speakers. I had González, Almunia, Borrell, then Almunia again; I had periods where there was no opposition speaker, and at the end of my term, in truth, I may as well not have had one at all. That was entirely in spite of my efforts, because I would have liked to have had a steadier relationship with the Socialists. When the PSOE went through the crisis that led to Rodríguez Zapatero being named their last General Secretary of my term, we refrained from commenting on the whole process. We didn't say a word.

I gave express instructions about it, and they were followed, because I thought it wasn't our place to start sticking our fingers in the opposition's wounds. Not everyone in the party shared my views, and some Popular Party members thought we were being too soft, too nice. I wanted to start off with a positive relationship and avoid jumping the gun in terms of criticism; I thought it would be a good idea to make things easier for the new General Secretary and let his party regain some stability. I had the impression that he was going to have a tougher time than me. That's what I told him. And I was right.

You can't slam the door behind you when you leave a party; you have to leave your house in order and your platform clear and well articulated. A party is not an organization that throws everything into winning an election and nothing into anything else, and it's certainly not a place for an obsessive desire for revenge. That has to be completely out of the question. Anyone who is obsessed loses the ability to think freely.

Parties should be prepared to be in power, and they should also be prepared to be in opposition. And to be able to be in opposition they have to have the authority to make pacts with the government in power. Otherwise you end up with an organization with no base and no structure. That's what happened with the Socialists. Now the PSOE seems like a confederation of parties. They can't offer serious, credible alternatives. They're constantly dealing with their internal balance of power.

When the last PSOE General Secretary stepped in, I thought we were going to be able to reach some type of consensus on certain basic issues. Then the Socialists changed strategy on the alternative to nationalism in the Basque Country. After that, they aligned with the United Left for the campaign against the Iraq War and the 2003 municipal elections. Now it seems they've convinced themselves that they'll win their share of power if, rather than maintaining consistent proposals and leadership throughout Spain, they ally themselves with nationalists and independents. This has led to a *national* party giving conflicting local statements to different communities. That shows a serious lack of judgment on important issues and a notable lack of global and historical perspective.

The Spanish system has some very odd practices and qualities that, I'm sure, will disappear over time. In Great Britain it would be unthinkable for the Prime Minister to meet up with the leader of the opposition for talks, except, of course, in Parliament. In Spain we've had some exceptional situations, such as the still recent creation of basic governmental institutions. But, barring exceptions such as war, I think that we in Spain tend to exaggerate the need for a close relationship between the Head of Government and the leader of the opposition. We seem to think they should be bowing and curtsying to each other constantly.

What I think matters is that everyone does their job. You might share certain viewpoints, some general goals for the country, but basically it's normal for majorities to form and for those majorities to function and the government to make its decisions based on the parliamentary majority that supports it and that the people elected. In Spain it sometimes seems that that majority has been elected on the condition that they don't try to work towards their agenda or carry out their platform. It's as if people think the majority should fulfill the minority's wishes, because the minority is actually the group with real legitimacy. And if you don't listen to the minority, then you don't know what democracy is. It's totally absurd.

There are two limits to consensus. The first is that you don't delegate your own responsibilities to the members of the consensus. You can't delegate your own job. And second, reaching consensus can never become the sole objective of political action. What you want to do is what matters. Once you know that, reaching consensus might be a valid instrument. But not always.

Besides, a consensus presumes that members have their positions straight. I might be willing to reach a consensus, because I've always believed in dialogue, but it's very difficult to reach a consensus with people who don't know what they want. Consensus is a political instrument we inherited from the UCD tradition. At the time it was a fundamental tool, one we needed to set the constitutional state in motion. If you understand political consensus in these terms, then it's clear that those taking part in it share some basic ideas, some important concepts and a historical perspective. Those efforts at consensus are important and without them things are much more difficult.

I've tried for consensus politics when dealing with crucial issues where I thought we could come to agreements. I was convinced, and I still am, that dialogue was critical and would be extraordinarily useful to achieve the economic stability we proposed. I carried on that course of action by renewing the Toledo Pact, for example, in 2003.

In December 2000 we initiated an anti-terrorist pact (the Pro-Freedom Anti-Terrorist Accord), although we had some serious differences of opinion, because the Socialists were not aiming for the same things as us. I wanted to draft an agreement that dealt with two types of issues: first, the struggle against terrorism, which was very specific; and second, the creation of a new type of politics that took the regional nationalist problem into account, which is a more long-term issue. The second issue is the one that was trickier to deal with the Socialists on. It seems that the PSOE gives more importance to tactical agreements that will keep them covered in the elections than they do to actual, meaningful agreements. This is something we should take up again and, obviously, something I want to do. We've always made it easy to comply.

The State Agreement for Justice Reform we signed in May 2001 has been broken. And it's been broken for entirely gratuitous reasons, as proved by the split by the Basque Nationalist Party and the United Left, who refuse to accept Supreme Court sentencing in the Basque Country. There was no reasonable argument to support that stance. The agreement has always been in the works and it's been taking shape for some time. We've renewed the electoral system, reformed the Finance Ministry statutes, introduced criminal justice reforms, changed the Civil Code and done everything in our power to make sure the courts have the personnel and the materials they need. Clearly, the agreement's aims are being fulfilled, with or without the Socialists on board. But it still would have been better for them not to break the agreement. I can't understand why a party that claims to want to govern puts an end to an agreement of this sort.

At any rate, Spain's justice system has seen considerable progress over these years. I firmly believe, as I always have, that a free society cannot last if it doesn't respect the law. Justice reforms are aimed at improving the system, and at getting our citizens to see that the law must be respected. We can't show those who don't follow the law any signs of weakness, especially in a country like ours that has become so prosperous that it's become an attractive place for organized crime.

We have to use common sense, the same common sense that tells us that teachers can't educate properly if they lack the authority to enforce the rules of civilized society. I wish we could have reached an agreement with the opposition on that, too, although pact or no pact we have, in these eight years, helped create a democracy comparable to that of any developed nation in the world.

CHAPTER FOUR

The Nation's Progress

When we came into office in 1996 we knew we were inheriting a difficult situation. The Socialists' last term, from 1993 to 1996, had been a terrible one. In a few short years, they'd managed to amass a whole collection of scandals. There were the Banesto scandals, the KIO scandal, the Grand Tibidabo scandal, the Filesa scandal, the Ibercorp scandal, and then the Gabriel Urralburu scandal in Navarra and the Manuel Ollero scandal in Andalusia. Even the Civil Guard General Director and the head of the Bank of Spain were implicated in serious corruption cases. It wasn't just a few bad apples placing their personal interests above those of the State. No. Unfortunately, it was a lot more serious than that.

Spain had become a platform for a way of seeing and doing things that derived from how the Socialists viewed society and the role of the state. They had no concept of budgetary control or why it was important. They saw the Administration as a tool for intervention in the national economy, which is the same as saying it could interfere in people's lives. The boundary between the public and the private was blurry at best. And that's where the seed of corruption lay, as we saw clearly from the last years of the PSOE government.

We have to keep in mind that the Socialist victory in 1982 was a sea change and not just a swing of the political pendulum. And what's more, Spain prospered for it, no doubt about that. Later came two very important events that clarified what happened. The first was in 1989. After the December 1988 general strike, the government caved in and decided to let what they called "the joys of social harmony" flow freely.

That led to incalculable spending increases, and the country couldn't handle it. The lack of budgetary control was unsustainable, and the government resorted to two schemes. The first was to try to get Spain into the European Monetary System as quickly as possible, so the currency would be under control. And the second was to keep the peseta at an artificially high exchange rate. Those two measures, rather than helping matters, aggravated the situation. Between 1992 and 1993 the country went into a serious recession. If you add to that all the corruption issues, it's pretty hard to see those years in a positive light.

In 1995 we saw worldwide economic recovery, which of course helped Spain, too. During the last phase of their government, the Socialists introduced measures to correct the economic policy they had followed until then. These were put in place, but they were only attempts to bridle a situation that was out of control.

On Not Giving Up

So, what did we think about this? First, we were convinced that Spain had what it took to prosper and move forward. Second, we were out to prove that it was possible to both respect the law and, at the same time, achieve our growth objectives with less government intervention in the economy. In other words, we were going to show that the more austere the state and the freer the economy, the less room there was for corruption and the more for progress. That was the number one aim of our fight against corruption, that and restoring faith in public life. The justice system could take care of punishing the wrongdoers; that wasn't our concern.

Rodrigo Rato was destined to have an extraordinary, brilliant role in this. Rato has a superb track record in economic matters and great political authority that derives from his skills and his role in the Popular Party over the years. He also has proven negotiation skills. We've always been very close, politically. And we agreed in our diagnoses of the situation at hand, and on what had to be done to remedy it.

We were convinced that Spain had taken three important steps in the last forty years. First, the Stabilization Plan at the end of the Fifties opened up the Spanish economy and gave way to a long period of development. Then came the 1977 Moncloa Pacts, which helped stabilize the economy. And finally came Spain's entry into what was then called the European Community, which brought Spain into a larger market and forced increased liberalization.

The next step had to be taken in the Nineties, with Spain's entry into the first stage of the Euro. To be in shape to join we had to leave behind fundamentally interventionist politics and substitute them for economic liberalization policies. We followed a course of action others had taken before us, but we set out to cover ground the Spanish economy had never touched before.

There's a quote from those years that people often take out of context. It's the famous, "Go, Mr. González," which I said to the Head of Government during the State of the Nation Debate in April 1994. The whole sentence was, "Go, Mr. González, and appoint someone else in your party as Prime Minister." I wasn't asking Felipe González to call general elections, nor did I want to delegitimize the government. The PSOE had the electoral support needed to rule and that has to be respected. What I was trying to say was that Felipe González could no longer rule the country given the corruption scandals and the shipwrecked economy. What he should have done was let someone else from his party take charge of the government. What I was proposing was that he save the country from the disaster it had become.

I knew he wouldn't listen to me. What's more, I always suspected he'd run again in 1996. We'd known since 1982 that Socialist rule was here for some time. The Socialists themselves thought it would be even longer than we did. They were talking about twenty or twenty-five years in office. At that time, in 1996, their years in power had turned them into some bizarre combination of Mexico's Institutional Revolutionary Party and the Swiss Social Democrats. They

liked to justify their economic policy by saying there was no alternative to what they had done. That it was the "only" way. The only economic policy was the one that the PSOE government was following.
Anything else would lead the country to ruin.

It was bizarre, because they were encouraging the country to give
up and at the same time not providing any real leadership. When we
got into office, everyone – including the Socialists – assumed we
wouldn't be in the Euro's first phase. They said it was nothing to be
surprised about, because Italy and Great Britain wouldn't be there,
either. Sometimes people even claimed that the Euro was an
unrealistic project, that would never get off the ground.

Spain had been classified as part of what some northern and
central European countries called "Club Med," as if Mediterranean
countries, and in particular Spain, were incapable of the economic
and budgetary discipline needed to join the Euro. The Maastricht
Treaty established the criteria for inclusion in 1992. That was the guarantee that the central European nucleus put in place to ensure the discipline of potentially irresponsible countries, especially those in the
south. Some people even thought that the stability pact would serve
to exclude certain countries. Ours, for example.

When we held a Spanish-Italian summit in Valencia in 1996 they
suggested the possibility of southern European countries, particularly
Spain and Italy, banding together, abstaining from the Euro at first and
then joining in the second phase. I said: no way.

Austerity and Deregulation

We had a completely different philosophy. We decided to do everything in our power to be one of the first countries to join the Euro.
We were well aware that this was a historic opportunity. We'd joined
the European Union late. Our entry into NATO was delayed. It
seemed that in European matters we were permanently destined to be
running behind.

The single currency was probably the most important thing to have happened in the European Union since the Community's creation under the 1957 Treaty of Rome. And we had the chance to participate in this historic event, to be key players. There was no way we were going to let that opportunity slip by. We had to do everything we possibly could to meet the criteria on time.

The outlook wasn't good. We had to fulfill certain conditions to be one of the founding member countries of the European Monetary Union as well as the Maastricht Treaty's five criteria, and in mid-1996 we only met one: exchange rates. We had to meet the inflation target (less than 2.7%), long-term interest rates (under 7.8%), government budget deficit (less than 3%) and public debt (which had to be less than 60% of the GDP). We had to do all of that in a very short space of time, between May 1996 and December 1997, and have an inspection during the last year. It was an incredibly tight deadline.

Our economic priorities stemmed from our decision to try to join the Euro. First came restraints on public spending. We froze public sector pay, reduced recruitment and employment offers and checked budget increases, which had to be below the economy's real growth rate. We knew we were asking a lot, but we were also convinced that these sacrifices would bear fruit and that we'd see results very quickly.

Then in June 1996 we set a whole slew of deregulation measures in motion to encourage competition in the Spanish economy. Here we actually found ourselves ahead of Brussels' requirements so we didn't need certain extensions that had been granted, like the one they'd given us to deregulate telecommunications. We subjected professional bodies to legislation on competition and deregulated prices. We deregulated cell phones and regulated cable television. Spain became one of the most open countries in the electricity sector and we opened up the air transportation market. We couldn't modify the restrictive trade law implemented by the PSOE government in 1985 because the Catalan nationalist party Convergencia i Unió wouldn't let us and the Autonomous Communities control this matter. And we also hit roadblocks deregulating land ownership. A Constitutional Court ruling that the PSOE pushed through banned us from doing what we wanted to, which was to have green belt land classified solely according to environmental and landscape criteria.

That's the way politics goes. I had hoped for complete deregulation, but as it stands what we achieved overall were the most important deregulation measures in Spain's recent history. You can still feel the effects today. For example, if Madrid is one of the most prosperous Autonomous Communities in the country, that might be because Madrid's trade is more deregulated than other Communities'.

Along with budgetary control and deregulation we also privatized, as a natural result of our deregulation measures. It wasn't an attempt to pay off debts or hide the deficit while controlling private industry. That's what Socialists did. What we wanted was to privatize in order to make the economy dynamic, while retaining a modicum of state ownership in some cases.

What we did was float companies that could be privatized immediately, like Argentaria, Repsol, Enagás, Endesa and Telefónica. Then we privatized companies that were still public, like Aceralia and Tabacalera; and finally we floated companies like Iberia and Santa Bárbara. Today all that remains to be privatized are a few particular companies in sectors that require special treatment, such as mining and dock work. The rest – telecommunications, transportation, energy – are all privatized.

Once companies are privatized, they make their own management decisions; they decide their aims and their strategies. There are companies where I don't even know the CEO's name. Privatization required transparency and it also required solvent, professional businesspeople to take over executive positions. We were looking for good managers.

When we came to power, they said privatization would never work. They even said – literally - that we should sell Iberia for one peseta, just give the airline away. Today it's a profitable company, so that would have been a bad move. We were convinced that all of those companies could run efficiently, competitively, and profitably.

And we were right. The state earned a lot of money, too, much more than initially predicted. That facilitated the process, but what mattered was that every time one of these companies had an IPO they covered the cost of flotation, proving yet again that the public had both the resources and the confidence in the Spanish economy.

I've had some problems in Europe as a result of our privatization, because not everyone went through with it. And as a result, Europe has a single market, but it's fragmented. There are protected zones, with state controlled public enterprises, and other zones that are not protected and where companies compete without the support of their governments. That's unfair, and it's unfaithful to the agreements made. It has to be fixed. But what we had to do at the time was follow through with our program and achieve greater efficiency.

Austerity measures, deregulation and privatization allowed us to embark on a new taxation policy in Spain. It can be summed up very simply: lower taxes. That was the 1999 fiscal reform when we lowered income tax by 13.7%, and approximately five million people became exempt from filing taxes.

That was another electoral campaign taboo. They had said that we couldn't do anything about taxes, especially not manage to lower them without increasing the deficit. Well, we did. When the state stops siphoning off the economy's resources, the economy grows and state revenues increase. We also introduced labor reform and, thanks to politics aimed at social harmony, we obtained salary increases.

All this meant we went through some intense changes. We also regained our confidence. In 1995, our national risk premium was at about 600 basis points. Today it's zero. Spain is solvent and trustworthy.

Against all predictions, in December 1997 we entered the Euro in the first phase. That proved that there was a serious, credible alternative to Socialist politics, to what they claimed was the "only" way. There was no reason to lose hope and certainly no need for any inferiority complex. We had proven ourselves and could stand tall amongst the big European countries.

The End of Socialism

I've always been interested in liberal economic ideas. I'd read Lucas Beltrán, one of the great Spanish economists, and Ramón Carande, though more as a historian. I'd met Enrique Fuentes Quintana, who had helped open up the Spanish economy in the Sixties and then had a role in the Moncloa Pacts during the transition. I also knew and had read Juan Velarde Fuertes. In the Popular Party I was friendly with a group of economists that included Rodrigo Rato and, later, Cristóbal Montoro. What they all have in common is that set of ideas and convictions known as economic liberalism.

I've always believed that the richer and stronger a country, the less its government intervenes and the more stable its institutions and respect for the law. That's what governing is all about: making sure the rules are followed. That's where liberal convictions about autonomous society and the moral primacy of individual freedom intersect with political vocation.

In addition to that, the idea that liberalization is superior to socialism is borne out by practice. It was obvious to anyone who could see that interventionist policies don't get you anywhere. Not in real socialism, as seen in communist regimes, and not in the socialism that the PSOE put into practice here. Here there were no budgetary controls, no spending restraints, and no clear idea of how to differentiate society from the state.

Liberalization policies and austerity measures, on the other hand, had worked. Practice had shown that liberalism was the way to go. That was what the economic policies of the Eighties in the US showed. They confirmed that the demand-driven economic policies that had prevailed in a good part of Western economic policy in the Sixties and Seventies had failed.

I had the chance to meet Margaret Thatcher on two separate occasions. The first was my first European Democratic Union meeting; at the time the Popular Party had not yet joined the European Popular Party. It was in Helsinki, a few months after Thatcher had stepped down. I gave a speech on the security risks presented by Islamic fundamentalism and, when I finished, Thatcher made a passing comment, something along the lines of, "Finally I meet a Spanish politician who knows what's what."

We met again a couple of years later, when I was still in the opposition. We had an argument, because she asked me about the old Francoists in my party. She even used the word "fascism." Since I knew that she was in the habit of provoking people to see how they measured up, I replied that there were more of those in her party than in mine. Federico Trillo, who was present, didn't know where to look. But after having started out so aggressively, she ended up saying, "You and I are going to get along." And we did.

The fall of the Berlin Wall in 1989 proved that socialism had completed its historical cycle. It had run out of steam, it had nothing more to offer. That's what Francis Fukuyama was trying to say in his book *The End of History*. He didn't mean that history, the events that make up humanity, had ended. That's nonsense. What he was pointing out, and I think he's right, is that History, in the Marxist sense of the word, is over. It had been proven that there was no heaven on earth; no one could take the truth for granted and nothing can take the place of a society that knows what it wants. Fukuyama maintains something that to me is obvious: there are no alternatives to liberal democracy, which is the only type of government that can maintain an open, flexible economy in the long run. So it stands that liberal democracy is the best way to provide people with happiness and well-being.

Social Harmony

When I got to the Moncloa Palace after the 1996 elections there were no meetings called to deal with the transfer of powers. There was one lunch where Felipe González invited Adolfo Suárez, but not Leopoldo Calvo Sotelo, so the three of us talked for a little while. Felipe González told me I'd have to raise taxes. I disagreed and told him why

I thought just the opposite: that I needed to lower them.

I wasn't given anything: no documents, no reports, not a single piece of paper, in fact, which left us a little bemused. Then finally a piece of paper turned up. It was an incident report from the Civil Guard, documenting what had happened in the country that day. I read it with interest, as I imagine the Minister of the Interior continued to do everyday thereafter.

When I got into office I had no plans for revenge, no desire to expose what had been swept under the carpet, the way the Socialists said they would in 1982. In the first place, we in the Popular Party have always believed that continuity is fundamental to the governing of a country. All governments inherit situations from their predecessors, and though they might amend certain policies, they have to ensure there is no rupture, no split, and definitely no personal reprisals. Besides, I never saw the point of revenge. I still don't.

As I said, we didn't want to see what they'd swept under the rug. What we wanted was to air out the room, let in a fresh breeze. We wanted to go from a closed approach to the economy and the nation to one where economic agents were allowed to make their own decisions, autonomously, with no political intervention. When I first became Head of Government, people came to see me: businesspeople, executives, bankers. They asked for my opinion and sometimes they just about asked for my blessing to do certain things. I always told them the same thing, which was that their decisions didn't concern me. I'm concerned with strategic decisions that might affect the interest of the entire country or Spain's position in the world, but I don't care about things that relate specifically to one certain company, regardless of how important it is. That was what I wanted to get across. I wanted to introduce new legislation, follow the law, and give people opportunities. I was convinced that that would change the mood of the country.

That conviction gave me great freedom when it came to making economic decisions. I've never once felt the need to bow to the demands of special-interest groups trying to use their support as leverage. In fact, it's almost been the opposite. People who move in power circles never did us any favors when the Socialists were in power. They're just a small sector of the business elite, in part a product of easy money and the lack of discipline shown by those in office. They're a result of interventionist politics in the Spanish economy that they say corrects market defects. I'm not so sure. What I am sure of is that those sorts of policies make it a lot easier to grant favors than it is to collect on them.

I've never approved of any of that and before coming to power I never made any special efforts to be liked. I've always tried to treat everyone, including businesspeople, respectfully and equally. I haven't always succeeded. When we were in opposition there were a lot of serious arguments. In 1992, Carlos Solchaga, the Finance Minister, presented a convergence program and I told him it would last five months. I was right. But that didn't win me any friends or earn me any favors with certain executives.

I knew I couldn't count on those very same executives' support when the unions called for a half-day general strike against the government in 1992. At the time the Socialists, with Carlos Solchaga still as Finance Minister, wanted to launch what they called the Plan for Competitiveness, and they tried to get us to absorb the costs of a policy we disagreed with. I refused flat out, because it didn't seem logical for us to take on measures we didn't believe in.

That's about when the Family Business Institute came to see us, because we were opposed to some of the taxation measures the government wanted to take. They were neither fair nor advisable. And that's what I said at the meeting. What's more, I told them that we weren't there thanks to any of them, and that they could do what they wanted but we weren't going to support the policy. In other words, I wasn't especially well liked in opposition.

Just as we knew we were not going to defend certain business interests when in power, we were also eager to have a good relationship with the unions. I had been in contact with some unionists when I was in opposition, most notably Nicolás Redondo, and also with some Workers' Committees (CC.OO.) leaders. I was the first in my party to attend a Workers' Committees conference as well as a General Workers' Confederation (UGT) conference. I had a good relationship with Nicolás Redondo Sr., and one year he invited me to the General Workers' Confederation conference. He told me not to worry if people started to shout, and I said it didn't worry me a bit. And of course he was right; a few people did shout when we walked in. I was with Celia Villalobos and at the end, when people stood with their fists raised to sing the *Internationale*, Celia said, "What are we supposed to do now?" "Nothing," I said, "Just stand up and listen."

I had several confidential meetings with Nicolás Redondo. He's a sensible man, he has a great human quality and I'm always interested in his political opinions. He's helped me out in many ways. We ended up developing an intense personal relationship, which has carried on in his son, and I've also always had open dialogue with José María Fidalgo, who has an amazing ability to come up with interesting proposals. Antonio Gutiérrez and Cándido Méndez have also been there, and they've kept the channels of communication open without renouncing their convictions.

A lot of people were surprised that we had such a cooperative relationship with the unions; that's because they themselves were pigeonholed, stuck in their rigid positions. They said I would try to destroy the unions. They even said I would engage in the politics of rancor. As if I, having won the elections, would have any intention of enacting policies that would harm people. It was absurd. If anyone was feeling rancor, it was the party that had lost the elections.

I told the unions from day one that I was interested in the same politics I've always practiced: consensus politics. Dialogue is good for the country and I had no intention of persecuting anyone or dismantling any organizations. Instruments of consensus like unions, collective bargaining and national negotiations are very important, not least because they promote unity in the country as a whole. As long as the unions, too, were willing, I wouldn't have any prejudices at all.

And that's the kind of politics we engaged in. Leading things from the Ministry of Labor and Social Affairs was Javier Arenas, who signed the 1997 pact for labor market reform with the unions. His tenacity and capacity for dialogue are absolutely out of this world. He never gives up and his resolve was incredibly valuable to us then. First, because we had some very ambitious aims and any step in the right direction, no matter how small, was valuable. And also, because maintaining a healthy social climate, a climate of dialogue, was fundamental; we had to keep advancing with no setbacks, had to keep boosting our policies' credibility. If we needed to slow down or to apply other measures in exchange for a step in the right direction, we did. Better a short step towards the finish line than a big one in another direction. What really matters is accumulating lots of little steps, because the more things take shape the more confidence people have. That was what it was all about.

It's true that the unions called a general strike in June 2002 against our increased market flexibility reforms. But that strike had a political side and a social side. As far as the political side went, it was obvious that after three general strikes with the Socialists in power, there would have to be at least one called against us. And as far as the social side, the strike was a bit more complicated. The government always loses when there's a general strike. Always. Even if the strike is a failure. We asked ourselves what we could do to improve the atmosphere and regain the social harmony we'd always managed to preserve, ever since 1996. That was what mattered. We didn't renounce the measures that had been adopted. That was what we did after the summer, when we went back over some of the decisions that had led to the strike.

Politically it was a lost cause. As was to be expected, the unions took advantage of the government's decision to turn what had been a failure, at least a relative failure, into a political victory. I can't say I got what I wanted. But faced with the choice of following the measures we'd adopted or reopening the channels of communication and dialogue, which has been one of the keys to our success over these past years, I chose the latter. And I really don't regret it.

Balancing the Budget

When we got into office in 1996, our plans called for substantial reductions in government expenditure. That was part of a personal plan that I'd had since I started working on the party's economic program, and I've defended it ever since. I also took part in creating budgets and, as opposition leader, I had always taken part in the annual state budget debates in Parliament.

In the early days, we created a special Budget Office in the Prime Minister's Office, to gather information and keep on top of what each Ministry was spending. What we were trying to do was put pressure directly on those who were responsible for determining how much the government spent. They had to know that they were constantly being watched from the top. Professor José Barea, an excellent economist and a man I've always admired, presided over the office. We had to send a very clear message: this professor, a specialist in public spending control, a man respected in the University and in the Administration, and as feared as he is famous, is on the Prime Minister's side. Barea did a great job.

Then came the political authority of the Treasury and the Ministry of the Economy, both of which also had my support to cut all the spending they needed to. When they drew up their budgets, we decided where the cuts would come from. I helped with this personally. Once the decisions were made, there wasn't much room for discussion. They were simply put into action. Those were the figures and that's what we had to abide by. In just one short year, 1996, we reduced the deficit from 6.6% to 4.4% of the GDP.

But a balanced budget was a long-term objective. We needed discipline and, what's more, we had to establish a culture of budgetary discipline. There hadn't been a balanced budget since the start of the 20th century, under Fernández Villaverde. Azaña had tried to get the budget back on track and restructure the Treasury insofar as possible at that time, which wasn't saying much. What I wanted was to force Spain out of that lack of discipline, that laziness that had set in so long ago. That's why I kept insisting that nothing is free, that the money a government spends is always someone else's money, our people's money. We had to achieve once and for all what so many governments had proposed but never actually managed. And once we did, we had to keep it up.

We wanted our stability program ready for 1998-2002 and it's been updated since then. The basic measures it lays out include having Parliament approve a General Budgetary Stability Act and, moreover, introducing a culture of austerity and budgetary balance in public finance. We also changed the way budgets are presented. Parliament sets spending limits that the government cannot exceed and it also makes long-range projections. Now we can take long-term measures and government has to submit to much tighter controls. The days of budget excess as common currency are no more.

Spain is one of the most decentralized countries in the world. So establishing control mechanisms for the Autonomous Communities was also critical. For every 100 Euros spent, only 48 are spent by the national administration. The rest is spent by city councils and Autonomous Communities. That's why general discipline is so important and why everyone has to accept mechanisms for control. Each of the state's constituents ought to share the same objectives.

Changing people's mindset is vital. Now, Spaniards know that nothing is free. Ever. When the government spends, the people pick up the tab. So now I think we've come to understand that the state shouldn't spend more than it brings in, and that the less the state spends - provided it fulfils its responsibilities - the more prosperous everyone will be. That's how we managed to decrease state spending from 47% of the GDP in 1996 to 40% now. And that's how we balanced the budget and achieved the famous zero deficit, in 2001, and how we kept it up in the years that followed. In 2003 we actually had a surplus; that is, the revenue that came in was greater than what we spent. This is the longest period of balanced budget in Spain's history, and since the surplus goes to Social Security, state social services have a very bright future. That was why, in 2000, we created the

Social Security Reserve Fund, in compliance with the Toledo Pact, which we've continued to contribute to with those surplusses.

These days, experts and professors might debate about whether a certain level of deficit or debt is necessary at certain points in history. Frankly, that's a purely academic discussion. Outside of that, we've proven that when the economy starts to decline, as it did in 2000, a balanced budget and financial discipline let the country keep growing, generating employment and making foreign investments. Can you imagine what would have happened in Spain if, between 2001 and 2003, we'd had a deficit of 2% or 3% of the GDP? We would have gone into debt, economic activity would have been suspended and we'd be getting rid of jobs. We'd be right back where we were in 1993.

Luckily, no one seriously argues about the benefits of a balanced budget on general prosperity anymore. Now, every major party has incorporated balancing the budget into their platform because they know that voters understand its importance. So it seems that even the opposition has come on board on this issue.

Lowering Taxes

But we also had other objectives; we didn't just want financial discipline and public spending restraints. In fact, that was aimed at job creation, and beyond mere creation, at seeing full employment on the Spanish horizon. In order to achieve that, we needed the Spanish economy to grow until it caught up to the average European economy.

That was always what every Spanish government wanted to achieve, politically and economically, since the early Seventies when our economy began to open up. Every time we've opened our economy to foreign investment, Spain has grown and Spaniards have prospered. That's why we had to keep on in the same vein. Today we have one of the most open economies in Europe. We've gone from 47% to 58% aperture between 1996 and 2003. We get a lot of foreign investment because, although production costs in Spain have naturally risen, Spain has become a stable, legislatively secure, trustworthy country with a high degree of transparency, which translates to a lack of corruption. We're also a country that, for the first time in a long time, has started to invest abroad. Spaniards and Spanish businesses feel secure enough to take the plunge into foreign ventures and compete in foreign markets.

We've regained the entrepreneurial spirit, which is what a market economy is all about. Regardless of the political leanings of whoever first said it, we've always been told that a market economy is immoral because it's based on selfishness. They also used to say that a market economy is dangerous because it creates apparent wealth that benefits a few while leaving out the majority. I don't think it's that straightforward. A market economy is based on individual freedom, which is based in turn on responsibility.

The modern state has to ensure a certain amount of well-being and certain opportunities for everyone: universal healthcare coverage, pensions, quality education. But it doesn't have to interfere in people's freedom, because it can't take the place of people's individual responsibility for their actions. What it can do, in this respect, is guarantee a legal framework and institutions that allow that freedom to be exercised, and it can ensure that anyone acting outside of that legal framework is excluded from the game. That's what we had to do in Spain: give people back their confidence so they realized that they could take the initiative to better their own situation without negatively affecting society's general interests. When you work for your own benefit within a stable, transparent, safe institutional framework, you're benefiting everyone.

That's what a country's growth is based upon. As I've already said, we took austerity measures from the second we reached government. We also reduced the national debt by 18 points, from 68.1% of the GDP in 1996 to 50.1% in 2004. This alone saved the state, which is to say the Spanish public, 1,700 million Euros a year in interest payments alone.

That savings, and the reduction in public spending, is what allowed us to lower taxes. That was another taboo subject before we were elected. No one had dared to lower taxes because they said that the state would be left without the revenue it needed to function. That was what the Socialists said in the 1993 campaign, when they claimed we were going to leave senior citizens and retired people without pensions. As if someone attempting to govern Spain would aim to take away anyone's pension!

As soon as we got into office we started work on lowering taxes. First we reduced business taxes and stopped penalizing savings, because up until eight years ago in Spain you were punished if you set aside money for your retirement, or for your children, or to invest in a company. We also reduced inheritance tax, and then we set about eliminating estate tax in the Autonomous Communities where the Popular Party was in power.

Finally – and this takes us back to 1999 – came the high point of our policy, which was lowering income tax. By that time the accusations of getting rid of pensions had disappeared, because no one had lost a pension. We'd done all we promised. And since that argument didn't work anymore, they came out with one of those absurd arguments that the left likes so much. They said that lowering taxes was unfair because it would benefit the rich more and wouldn't benefit those who most needed it. We all know that taxes burden workers the most, those who work for a paycheck, the middle class. That's the vast majority of the country we're talking about, and they're the ones who bear the real burden of income tax.

Lowering taxes gives back money to that majority; it gives them back money that the state has been withholding. And that's what we wanted to do: give something back to society, something that there was no reason to withhold in the first place, something that was hurting people. When that huge middle class that makes up the vast majority of the country starts to understand, to see the difference in their paychecks, they also realize that they can use that money to invest in other things.

That's one of the things that led to growth in our economy. And, despite what they predicted, it also increased state revenue. Lowering taxes increases economic activity, and that increases revenue. That's a proven fact that it took the left a long time to come to terms with. These days, no one tries to deny it.

There is not a single party today that would campaign on a platform including a tax hike. They know no one would vote for them. And they know no one would vote for them not just because it's an unpopular measure, but because people have a different mind-set now.

That does present new challenges and new debates. We no longer have the same, stale debates about whether lowering taxes favors one group over another. That's demagogy. What matters is that the government guarantees equal opportunities and compliance with the law and that Spaniards know that their financial plans will not be penalized.

Full Employment: The Silent Revolution

We've made serious advances towards one of the historic objectives in Spanish politics: achieving income levels on a par with Europe. In 1996 we inherited a country where the average income was at 78% of the European average. We were a long way behind. They said we'd never reach European levels, that that was impossible, utopian. This term, utopian, by the way, is funny, because a lot of the very same people who told us that our aim was utopian also talk about utopia as if it were the only worthwhile aim in politics. But utopia or no utopia, in 2003 our figures were at 86% of the European average. So we increased by eight percentage points in less than eight years, when from 1976 to 1995 the country was stuck at 78.3%. In fact, the rate had even decreased a little, which is to say we'd actually moved farther away from European standards of living.

What made our advances possible was more than nine years of sustained growth. That's something rarely seen in Spanish history. There hasn't been such a long period of sustained growth in this country for quite some time. Between 1997 and 1999 the GDP increased by 4.2%. We surpassed other Western countries by more than one percentage point. In 1999 and 2000 our economy grew by 4.1%.

Here's something meaningful: the Spanish economy has now broken a performance pattern it seemed historically condemned to follow. When our European neighbors had growth periods, so did we, and at a faster rate. But when the economic cycle slowed and they stopped showing signs of growth, the Spanish economy would go into an even deeper recession. So, we'd both grow faster and recede further. That made it impossible to even think about reaching European convergence.

So, what we had to do was break a historic pattern. And that's what we did over the course of those years. Our growth rate surpassed that of other European countries in good cycles. But in the lean years after 2000, we didn't repeat our classic performance by entering a recession at a faster rate than other countries, or even at the same rate. We might have shown more moderate growth, but we still showed growth. Something in the range of 2.5%, when some of our other European Community member states like France and Germany either stagnated or went into a light recession. I don't want to lecture anybody, especially not countries with long and unblemished democracies and indisputable abilities to create wealth. What I want to highlight is that Spaniards have successfully turned a goal into a reality.

That means that our growth rate is not based on foreign capital, because our main trade partners, the countries we export most to, are now, for the most part, stagnating. Our recovery comes down to the Spanish economy's own ability to generate savings, investment, and economic activity. We've regained our self-confidence.

All of this has allowed us to realize our principal objective: increased employment that will finally let us reach full employment in 2010. The problem with the Spanish economy was not just that we had a high unemployment rate. In 1996 when we came into power, we had 23% unemployment, which translates into 3.7 million Spaniards out of work. The problem was also that in Spain, unlike in other European countries, fewer people worked because the economy had been unable to do anything about job creation. In 1975 there were twelve million people in work. More than twenty years later, in 1996, that figure had not changed; still only twelve million people were employed.

That had to change. We had to create jobs for young people, who were just entering the workforce. But we also had to increase the employment rates overall. That was a personal objective of mine, something I wanted to achieve or at least get on track so that we could work towards it in stages.

We had said it often enough, and even when they lectured us on social justice and the welfare state, we always had the same reply: we are not going to cut social services. Not only are we not going to cut them, we'll increase them.

When we got into office the Social Security system was bankrupt. In 1995 it had a deficit of 0.7% of the GDP, i.e. 500 billion pesetas. During our first months in power we had to borrow money just to pay pensions. Given the state that Social Security was in at the time, we couldn't even make it to the end of the month.

Today, Social Security is back on track. Since Spanish society has created jobs and thanks to the fiscal measures that forced a lot of illegal employment out into the open, we now have 16.6 million people making contributions, which is 4.3 million more than in 1996 when there were only 12.3 million paying in to Social Security. Thanks to that we now have a surplus and have fulfilled the Toledo Pact agreements as well as created a Social Security Reserve Fund to cushion the effects of economic downturn and guarantee that the pension system is financially balanced. Our objective for 2004 is to make sure that the Fund has over six billion Euros. We'll double the endowment.

In addition to complying with the Toledo Pact stipulations we've also sought consensus and commitment from all political forces to ensure that the general outlook for Social Security remains the same.

In October of the same year, 1996, we signed an important agreement with the unions on this. We've also increased pensions, particularly the lowest paying ones, in order to compensate for inequalities in the system. And we passed a law requiring government to commit to raising pensions every year to keep them in line with the cost of living increase.

We're convinced, though, that the most efficient social policy is also the fairest at the end of the day, and that is giving people a chance to work. There is no better social policy than assuring people that they'll be able to make plans and fulfill them, turn them into reality, take advantage of new opportunities arising in society. The public has to know that their efforts are not in vain, that it's worth it to struggle and take risks in order to get what you want.

So based on that idea we created 4.2 million jobs over the course of these past eight years. We went from 12.6 million employed in 1996 to 16.8 million in 2003. Half of those jobs went to women. That shows that we were right about getting that important sector of society who had been out of the labor market to join the workforce, it shows that it could be done. Although there's still a long way to go, women, whose initiative and effort had previously been limited to the domestic sphere, are now contributing to overall prosperity. Working at home is important, but so is letting women who want to work outside the home know that there are jobs for them, that they can bring money home to their families and have independence, too. I should also point out that for the first time in Spanish history, the leaders of both houses of Parliament are women: Luisa Fernanda Rudi and Esperanza Aguirre are both first-rate politicians.

I have sometimes referred to job creation as a social revolution. A silent, discrete revolution, but one that has profoundly changed life in Spain. It has let us get the Treasury, Social Security and public accounts back on track. It has given families more money and created opportunities for everyone, because greater prosperity also increases the chances of finding new sources of wealth, new demands and new ways to satisfy needs that didn't used to exist. Work provides freedom, confidence and personal autonomy.

In spite of what people have said, the more than four million jobs that Spanish society has created over these past years are not, for the most part, precarious. Quite the opposite. That was another one of our priorities when we came into office. Between 1987 and 1996 the number of fixed-term contracts decreased by nearly half a million, while temporary employment was up by 1.8 million. We had to do something about the trend towards precarious employment that had begun in the mid-Eighties. We had to reverse it and increase stable employment to the point where it surpassed temporary-contract jobs.

That's why in 1997 we introduced labor reform that had been agreed by consensus. The effects were immediate. That same year the trend began to change, with a 90% increase in hiring for stable jobs. The temp rate went from 33.5% in 1997 to 30.6% in 2003. And since 1996 the number of workers with indefinite contracts has grown by 3.3 million, which means that eight of every ten Spaniards hired in the last seven years has a stable contract. That's very important. With a stable job, people can make long-term plans, think about starting a family, having kids, and buying a house.

That's part of the silent revolution I was referring to earlier. And it's a good indication of the problems faced when it comes to job creation. The 1997 labor reform agreements included significant bonuses towards Social Security contributions for companies creating stable employment. That meant that they were very aware of the reduced labor costs for new hires. And I'm not just talking about big companies. I'm talking about family businesses, small companies, and those employing between one and ten people. Small- and medium-sized companies are the ones that create the most jobs when you add them all up.

The worst thing about temporary contracts isn't that they're temporary. In Spain, tourism is one of the most significant economic sectors, and seasonal employment is an important part of the industry. But what worries me about temporary positions is the uncertainty they create when hiring responds not to a clear necessity but to other factors. It's when workers are forced to renew limited contracts again and again, without ever having the chance at a stable job. That leads to people not being covered, and not having any security or any confidence, because people who are trapped in that system don't see any way out, any way to see their long-term prospects.

Well, these temporary schemes might be okay with some businesspeople and they might also be okay with the unions, despite what people think. But I doubt that they're okay with the workers themselves. And regardless, they also present another problem, which is not the labor costs but the cost of making the labor market itself flexible. The 1997 reform lowered compensation from 45 to 33 days worked per year. And that too, beyond any shadow of a doubt, helped in the creation of stable employment.

In Defense of Globalization

I'm a firm believer in globalization. Over the course of human history there have been great periods when the economy opened up: Spain's expansion into Latin America and the Far East; the industrial revolution; the years leading up to the First World War. Those are three periods when economies opened up beyond their borders, and they are times when we saw increases in overall prosperity.

Spain's experience in the last fifty years also shows that the more an economy opens up, the more the country progresses. We saw that in the Sixties, again in the Eighties, and we're seeing it again now, having definitively joined the global goods and services market.

Spain went from investing 0.1% of the GDP abroad in 1990 to investing 10% of it in 2000. And are Spaniards worse off now than they were then? I think the answer is obvious. Opening up markets has not harmed us; it's given us an opportunity that we showed we could take advantage of. Look at Latin America, for example. Between 1990 and 1995 we invested five billion dollars there. Between 1996 and 2000 we invested 105 billion. That's a huge sum. And it shows a willingness to take advantage of the opportunities that the opening up of Latin American economies provided us. It also shows a willingness to accept risk. Spain's investment in Latin America was a strategic decision, one that has really taken off during these past few years. We are the top European investor and rank second in the world in Latin American investment.

We have all benefited from this. We took advantage of these years of expansion very wisely. And new problems have arisen, such as being seen as an overwhelming superpower, and the possibility of that jeopardizing the current situation and future development. But when the situation changed, we stayed the course. That's what we had to do.

Now we've got another great opportunity in the markets of the new European Union countries. Spain could expand there, and we have a lot to offer. It's a different situation, because these countries are going to form part of a single market, so they'll be competing with us, too. But instead of complaining, we have to do whatever we can to take advantage of the new opportunities the situation presents us.

I once said that I refused to let Spain stop being an industrialized nation. And we haven't stopped. We have more businesses than ever, around 2.6 million, in fact. We export cars, food, machinery, transport materials and light industrial products. We can't lose that, although, obviously, we are evolving towards a service-sector economy. But there, too, we can export. In tourism, for example, where we have experience and know-how that can be marketed abroad.

Spain, however, has a very close network of small- and medium-sized businesses. Given their scope, they don't have much chance of exploring foreign markets. We've helped them as much as we can, but we have to keep helping them. We have to provide ways for them to join the information society and take advantage of all it has to offer. We have to make sure Spanish companies are increasingly competitive, although I think they've already managed that, and more than people think. We have to maintain a favorable social climate that allows companies to undertake strategic plans, whether large or small. What all this means is, we have to deepen and strengthen the climate of confidence we've created in these years.

If the basic axes that generate confidence are maintained, then the government can get to work on what is really its field: advancing security, justice, the armed forces and Spain's foreign interests. The two processes go hand in hand. One strengthens Spanish society's confidence and the other enhances the confidence that other countries have in Spain. If these two processes continue and feed off of each other, we can keep generating wealth, employment and economic activity. And that way we can keep health care coverage, education, pensions and social spending strong and healthy.

Social welfare can't be maintained by protectionist policies. Just the opposite, in fact. The protectionist arguments, in favor of closing economies to the alleged risks and theoretical foreign threats, always favor the rich and hurt the poor. A country's prosperity is what upholds the solidarity that social spending is based on. And that prosperity is directly related to an open economy.

Some people are still skeptical of open economies. Some countries prefer to be interventionist and keep their economies closed. They say that it's a demonstration of solidarity and cooperation. That's just not true. In cases like that, talk of solidarity is nothing more than a way to clear their consciences. Protectionism hurts those countries because they end up losing opportunities, and then their own citizens pay the price, and it's a high one: regulations, trade barriers and tariffs. In addition to hurting themselves, they also hurt less developed countries, because they impede their access to more wealthy markets, thereby holding them back from progress.

Protectionists – the anti-globalization gang – don't ask the people living in developing nations if they want a better life. They're not interested in that. Poverty, poor working conditions, and child labor…those are not just blemishes that can be stamped out by putting up barriers against the free movement of people, or free trade, or freedom of information. Protectionism is also not going to solve the threat of terrorism, which is not related to globalization or even poverty; terrorism, as we in Spain well know, does not stem from a bad economy. The only thing all of that achieves is forcing people to live in underdeveloped conditions that are far worst than those they'd have if they lived in countries with open economies.

But there is often an even worse corollary. With protectionism dressed up as anti-globalization in poor or underdeveloped countries, what you often end up with are corrupt oligarchies and opaque, non-democratic systems of government entrenched in power. When I say I'm in favor of globalization, I am also saying that without spreading democratic institutions that guarantee individual rights and their citizens' participation in political decisions, no country can take advantage of the opportunities of the open market. This is one of the great debates today, and it's not an easy one. Amongst other things, because if you want to encourage democracy in non-democratic countries, you have to be willing to help and to make the sacrifices that it seems many are unwilling to make.

Institutionalizing democracy is not easy. Nor is creating open, transparent markets with freely circulating information so that the highest possible number of people have access and can take advantage of opportunities. For instance, how can it be that countries with relatively small populations - oil-producing nations with raw materials, easy shots at big markets, potentially rich countries, to be blunt - have such high indices of poverty? Adam Smith would say that it's because their principal source of wealth, in this case oil, is in the hands of the government. He'd also say that wealth is generated when laws, private property and competition are respected.

Some people brand the desire to spread prosperity and democracy as imperialist. That's not how I see it. I don't see why it's imperialistic to work towards prosperity for all, especially in underdeveloped countries. Nor do I think the desire for countries to share the values that uphold world democracy is imperialistic. Individual freedom, responsibility, equal opportunities and participation in political life are not exclusively Western values. They are universal values that everyone can share. Putting them into practice is the only thing we can do today to guarantee peace and world order.

That's the challenge we now face.

Confidence is the key to being able to tackle these new challenges the right way. It's reasonable for people to feel suspicious at the thought of their cultural identity and their customs disappearing. But Spaniards have learned a lot about this over the years, too. When truly rooted in people's lives and minds, ways of life are never in danger - not even threatened - by joining a global market and areas much larger than the domestic sphere. These days, Spanish cultural traditions, regardless of type, show a level of vitality that just a few years ago many people thought impossible.

A Debt-Free Country

In our second term, after the 2000 elections, we set big packages of economic measures in motion. One at the start of the term and the other in 2002-2003. We also lowered income tax for the second time. We got rid of the Economic Activity Tax and Estate Tax. And we started the 2002-2007 infrastructure plan, which is where a lot of the great initiatives taking place now originated. It's very ambitious and it has continued and expanded what we had done up to now; it also took advantage of the results of the policies put into practice in our first term. We kept practicing consensus politics. We signed a pension agreement with the Workers' Commissions and renewed the Toledo Pact almost unanimously.

A government should guarantee equal opportunities and solidarity, and should promote the country's modernization. Over the years, we have maintained that equal rights should apply to everyone all over the country. There shouldn't be any difference between pensioners just because they live in different parts of the country. We put the national hydrology plan into action, which was an act of practical solidarity and historic necessity. We pushed through a very ambitious infrastructure plan, which is vital to modernizing the country and is transforming our landscape with its highways, freeways and high-speed trains. We've also tried to increase access to the Internet, so all Spaniards can get on-line. And we thought it was vital to encourage mobility both in education, with the single university district, and in the workforce.

The way our economy has overcome the crisis shows we were right. A lot of European countries have come through the crisis with almost zero growth. Not us. We've kept growing, kept up job creation. There is no better proof that our budgetary measures, austerity measures and liberalization and flexibility reforms were more than a personal obsession.

At first some people said that balancing the budget was an obsession with us. The Spanish economy could handle the deficit; we could raise taxes and spend freely. Meanwhile, we'd better divvy up the jobs that already existed because, they claimed, it was impossible to create more. It was an absurd way of looking at things. We said no, across the board. There was no reason to give up and give in.

The result is that now nobody talks about whether it's possible to balance the budget. Everyone knows it is. And that it's good for the country. Now, rather than arguing about the budget deficit, we argue about what to do with the surplus. Because since 2003, state budgets have not been in the red, they've been in the black.

We lowered taxes in our first term. We lowered them again in the second term. We've increased state social services. We've created a Social Security Reserve Fund to help guarantee our senior citizens a dignified future. And our books are not only in order but showing a surplus at a time when the economy is showing a downturn all over.

For us, it's obvious that increasing social services even more than we already have is not the right way to spend the surplus. The money saved up for Social Security shouldn't be spent now. What we need to do is save it for a rainy day so social services can be guaranteed in the future. And we have to keep working towards a framework that will guarantee pensioners that their retirement income will be increased each year and not be depleted by an irresponsible government. You can't go for political opportunism on something like this, spending today only to discover that tomorrow we have to lower the pensions of those who've worked all their lives to make up for it.

We proved we were right when we proposed that a real political alternative existed, that it was possible and that it would benefit the country as a whole.

The more flexible the Spanish economy is, the better the forecast for the future. It'll be better for us, just as it was better for the 15-member Europe, and will be better when there are ever more member states in the European Union. Spaniards will have more opportunities and initiative, the economy will show more growth and be more able to compete. Instead of being afraid of globalization, we can take advantage of the opportunities it offers.

That's the change I want for Spain. Today in Spain there are millions of shareholders who wake up every day knowing what it means to have a market economy and knowing what it means to get dividends. Four and a half million more people are now employed, and now have the chance to buy a home; that's a chance they didn't used to have, and we can't forget that. The housing market is dynamic. There's no doubt that the cost of housing is high, especially because land legislation in Spain is flawed, but it's also true that demand is high, and that comes from the social changes we've seen over the past few years.

We've made it easier to buy property. Mortgage rates are low, there are special tax deductions, there is incentive for first-time buyers and for young couples looking to buy a home. There are also a lot of foreigners who come to Spain, sometimes for a month and others indefinitely, who stay twenty-five and thirty years. Many of them buy property here. That's a show of confidence. During a visit to the US, Homeland Security Chief Tom Ridge, who used to be Governor of Pennsylvania, told me that people in his state move to Florida when they retire. He didn't like that, but he said he had to admit it was great for Florida.

We can now count on stability, on the fact that we are back on track. We'll have to keep taking initiatives of course, because there's always room for additional reform, but we're no longer at the same starting gate. We're not an old country with no credit anymore, we're not untrustworthy anymore; we're a modern, disciplined nation that keeps up its end of the bargain and complies with norms and agreements. To a certain degree we're even a model nation. We've put in a lot of years of hard work, a lot of years of uphill battle. And we have to keep on working.

CHAPTER FIVE

Spain's Role in the World

On September 11, 2001 I was on an official state visit to Estonia. That was in the run-up to Spain's presidency of the European Union, and we had decided to pay a visit to the countries that were about to join; we were in the Baltic States for a few days at that time. The afternoon of September 11th I was meeting with Estonia's Prime Minister. Suddenly, we were informed that there were pictures of the Twin Towers on fire being broadcasted on television. We interrupted our conversation to go and find out what had happened; there had been an attack. We gave a press conference condemning the terrorist act and suspended the rest of the trip, deciding to return to Madrid immediately.

A lot of people have asked me if I had thought, then, about the attempt on my life made in 1995. I thought about the people who were passengers on the hijacked planes, the people who were inside the Twin Towers, and what all that meant. The 1995 attack didn't change my personal views on terrorism or my political standpoint on what terrorism means. Nevertheless, surviving an attack has changed the way I approach certain things. Since then I've been more aware of what the loss of innocent life means, of what it means for people to lose their friends and families in a terrorist attack, as they did on September 11th.

I feel personally responsible, as Head of Government, for making sure that people who have suffered the effects of terrorism are taken care of. That's why I insist that the victims matter more than anything else, that what counts is giving them the strength to hang in there and recover. That's why I've tried to really be there for people who have terrorist threats against them or who've suffered attacks. And it's also what's crystallized my views on terrorism. We all have the right to decide what we believe in and to put forward different solutions, even to appeal for dialogue. But since then, since 1995, I know exactly what terrorism is.

September 11th

Just after the September 11th attacks there was tremendous confusion; but as soon as it became clear that a terrorist attack had taken place and as soon as people realized its magnitude, it was obvious that history would never be the same again. Analyzing the consequences of the attack and the possible political responses was crucial. For two reasons, everything would depend on the political decisions made in those moments.

First, what had previously been only a risk had now materialized into a brutal, cruel reality. Massive terrorist attacks like September 11th had been foreseen as a theoretical possibility. But now that theory had been put into practice. The second reason is that the attack had been against the United States, the leader. And attacks on the leader are always earth shattering.

From a strictly Spanish point of view, September 11th had very important consequences. We had often felt alone in the fight against terrorism. Too often people thought it was a local problem and, formal declarations aside, we were somewhat neglected because of other people's lack of understanding of the true scope of terrorism. Now was the time to take a step forward, both from a European perspective and vis-à-vis an international political stance on terrorism. The time had come for Spain, having flown the flag against terrorism for years, to take a resolute stance, one that left no room for question.

I was sure that the international community would offer an immediate and spectacular show of solidarity. Each country would endeavor to be more earnest than the last. I knew everyone would rush to see who got there first, who made the greatest gesture. Then, almost immediately, would come the backlash; we'd very quickly see who was *not* actually willing to shoulder any responsibility.

I didn't want to be in the initial race to show support because I was absolutely convinced that the time would come when the race would grind to a halt and the lack of subsequent action would set in. I made a public appearance: I spoke to President Bush immediately and sent a card to express my solidarity. But it wasn't until November that I flew to Washington.

Then came the intervention in Afghanistan. The overthrow of the Taliban, which was backed by the international community, derived from the logic of the attack and the subsequent show of solidarity. But it wasn't until later, until the intervention in Iraq, that all of the effects of September 11th began to be seen. And that's where the chain of solidarity started to show weak links. I didn't know when it would happen, but I knew sooner or later it would. And it was in the discussions on Iraq.

Solidarity and Responsibility

Meanwhile, it was important to make the most of this as a means of extending our international position in the fight against terrorism. We changed all of our counter-terrorist legislation, something we'd been planning to do for a long time. At my first European Conference, in Florence in June 1996, I had suggested, as had some previous governments, abolishing extradition proceedings within Europe. That was the first thing I put on the table, and we advanced slowly and with difficulties, which were later resolved. Some countries claimed certain constitutional problems, but everyone behaved sensibly and was receptive to changes in the legislation. No one had serious objections, not even the United Nations. Of course, translating United Nations law into action later was another matter.

There is a simple explanation for the difference between the initial solidarity shown and the lack of action and unwillingness to follow-up that came later. It's easier to understand if you keep in mind not only the politics involved, but also clichés and anti-Americanism. Once the first show of solidarity faded, questions about the motives behind the September 11th attack arose. And then came the temptation to explain the causes behind it, as if there were some explanation that could possibly make terrorism comprehensible. There were even some who attributed responsibility for the attack to the victims, i.e. blaming the United States.

There were a few highbrows in Spain who came out with that opinion, even to the point of making utterly ridiculous statements the very next day. They were saying things like, "The whole world shudders, waiting on tenterhooks to see how Bush will respond." At the time, they didn't even know how many thousands of people had died in the Twin Towers. Figures were saying there could be twenty, thirty, even fifty thousand people dead. But the world wasn't shuddering about that. They were worried about Bush's response. That's why it was clear from the beginning what was going to happen.

Here in Spain we've dealt with that phenomenon, too. There have been people who claim to understand terrorist actions and claim that the fight against terrorism can't be won. That's when they make appeals for dialogue rather than for the defeat of terrorism. There's a long hazy period, but in the end people's true intentions come to light. And after September 11th it came out in anti-Americanism. It's easy to show solidarity when there's a tragedy, but it's much harder to actually shoulder some responsibility when it comes time to act. And that's when we started to see the prejudices come out, prejudices that led us to the situation we ended up finding ourselves in.

Supporting the Iraqi Invasion

People are anti-American for several reasons. The first one comes out of what is an obvious truism: whoever is in power is not popular. Especially whoever is in charge of the world's greatest superpower. When Spain was a world leader, Spaniards weren't exactly popular. That was when the Black Legend was begun, claiming we were cruel, arrogant, haughty, proud. And that stuck for centuries. The English and the French, too, were unpopular when they were great world powers. And now the Americans are getting the same treatment.

In addition, in Europe it's politically correct to be anti-American. It's ridiculous, especially when Europeans deign to lecture everyone else, as Jean-François Revel says. We can't forget that, in the 20th century, especially the first half of the 20th century, European problems all came from Europe. The First World War was brought on by Europeans, as was the Second. Communism and Fascism are both problems originating in Europe. A good part of the problems in underdeveloped countries stem from conflicts and ideas born in Europe and exported from Europe. So it's absurd to lecture a country like the United States, which for over two hundred years has been stable and had strong democratic institutions.

Anti-Americanism is born of a European complex and of prejudices arising from the First World War. When the War ended, Europe was no longer in the position to make decisions for the rest of the world. The Second World War only reinforced that reality, and in spite of having been victorious, Great Britain was one of the first countries to realize it. That's why Britain built up the so-called "special relationship" with the United States and goes to great lengths to make sure they don't jeopardize it.

During the Cold War anti-American sentiment was more latent, because Europeans were dependent on the United States to protect them from the Soviet threat. But as soon as the Berlin Wall fell, that all changed. It was a historical triumph for the US: they dismantled an empire without firing a single shot. That's when the US emerged as the superpower, and that's why a lot of European countries made a grave error: with the Soviet threat removed, they thought there were no more threats. So they let their guard down, they disarmed. This resulted in a growing distance vis-à-vis the United States as far as security apparatus and capabilities were concerned, because the US hadn't jumped to the same conclusions as Europe. They understood that the end of the Soviet Union didn't mean the end of conflict and threats. But by the time Europe caught on, it was too late.

By that time, the new threats that emerged after the collapse of the Soviet Union had become a reality. There's international terrorism, which is capable of creating autonomous, self-sufficient cells and networks that are nearly impossible to keep track of, like Al-Qaeda. There's the proliferation of weapons of mass destruction, and there are reckless, lawless countries. Those three things combined are extraordinarily dangerous.

Islamic fundamentalism poses another threat. Now, it's not that Islam itself is a threat to world order. But there is no doubt that the Islamic world is fighting a battle between fundamentalist and more moderate tendencies. And it's a battle that hurts the Arab world first, because they're the ones suffering from attacks by radical fundamentalists. But the West is also in their sights; it's clear that Islamic fundamentalists have declared war on the West. Not just on the US, on the entire Western world. And they attacked the US because they are the leaders of the Western world. September 11th is the most obvious expression of that war, regardless of the people in Europe trying to claim that it has nothing to do with them and that it only affects the United States.

There is no doubt that the United States is the greatest liberal democracy in the world, and there are a lot of people who don't like either liberalism or democracy. They don't like liberalism and they hate a free economy. That's the mentality that justifies the European prejudices about the evil North American system.

But Spain's decision to support the United States in the war against terror in no way changes our position. We haven't suddenly become anti-Europe and pro-United States or pro-Atlantic. There's not a European Europe and an Atlantic Europe. They're both the same thing. From a Spanish perspective, we had been taking steps in the right direction and we'd always been supported by a broad consensus. Spain had joined the European Union and NATO. We had good relationships with our fellow member states and we were respectable but we weren't committed enough. For example, we hadn't joined NATO's military forces. I never thought that was right.

So that's where we were at the time of September 11th. And then the circumstances gave us the opportunity to change the state of play and make our international position the same as what we wanted domestically. A decision of that nature first required a personal commitment, because it has to rest on personal convictions. It's also a personal leadership decision, which in this case meant being determined to take on certain responsibilities. But it stops being a personal issue when the entire government backs it. It also stops being personal when an entire party supports the position, and when citizens confirm their support at the polls, as they did in the municipal and autonomous elections in May 2003. Then it's no longer a personal position; it's a stance that's been taken. And our position on Iraq stemmed from a defense of vital national interests.

In the last two hundred years, Spain has not shouldered international responsibilities or shown much interest in economic matters, particularly the global economy. After Napoleon's disastrous invasion of Spain, we were expelled from European politics at the Congress of Vienna in 1815. From then on, with rare exceptions, Spain has taken refuge within its own borders.

In 1978, things started to change. We started taking the necessary steps: we joined NATO and the European Union; we had a Mediterranean and North African policy. And all of this was done consensually, although I should add that we weren't always told the truth. Actually, what we were being told was that we were a second-rate country. That the best thing to do would be to follow the crowd, try to do well, but not draw attention to ourselves. And that's what changed: the willingness to step up and take on responsibilities.

The way I see it, this stems from two things. First is Spain's own position, which is now stronger and more central. And second are government decisions. Before our democracy we didn't exist on the world map. And now we do. That's what I was talking about when I said, "I don't want Spain to get stuck on the way to History." I understand that it's hard to adapt to such profound change in such a short time, especially with a relatively isolationist history behind us. When the photo from the Azores Summit was published, the one that showed me with Bush and Blair in March 2003, a lot of people thought, "What are we doing there? Why us?"

But there is a historic precedent for the Spanish decision to support the US. In 1998 the United States and Iraq had a very tense period, and the US government was on the verge of intervening militarily. That's when Clinton was in office; it's important to remember that the Iraq issue is not something Bush or the Republicans made up. Anyway, Clinton phoned me to ask for my support at the time. Then, the US government went public with a declaration of support from European countries like the United Kingdom and Spain. But before that, when Clinton called me, I said that I thought the time had come to take a stance, and I added that international law had to be respected and that we would support a US strategy based on UN resolutions, which is what I've always said. And that was our course of action.

We supported the Iraq intervention because Saddam Hussein's regime did not meet UN resolutions and he never showed the least bit of willingness to cooperate with weapons inspectors who were there to verify whether he had destroyed arms and halted weapons of mass destruction programs.

Clinton, Bush and Blair: Allies

I always had a good relationship with Clinton. He's an extraordinarily nice man and whenever I see him, it's a real pleasure to have a chance to talk and exchange information. But it's also true that, although we always had a very positive relationship, it wasn't as close as my relationship with some other leaders. Tony Blair, for example. Blair is a Clintonite, all the way. He's a great communicator, he's affable, like Clinton, and Bill Clinton was one of his great friends. But when the US elections came, the baton was passed and Blair has been successful in his leadership role with a new American President. Blair didn't act out of friendship or sympathy but by virtue of his convictions and his country's strategic interests. That shows that some countries have a historic continuity that the whole world respects when it's their turn to rule.

It was easy for me to strike up a friendship with Tony Blair. It's a generational thing: we're the same age. And since his first visit to Spain, during the Easter vacations in 1997, we've had a close, personal relationship based on mutual respect and friendship. And then there were other, more general factors. I've always been very much in favor of staying the course with Atlantic politics. I've always believed in the Atlantic link. I agreed entirely with Great Britain's policy on that, and their Atlantic interest is even greater than ours. I've talked to Blair quite a bit about Great Britain's historic position and about Spain's historic position at the turn of this century, and that has brought us together, because we fundamentally agree on what each of our courses should be. Besides, I like the Anglo-Saxon social and economic model. I'd like to be able to say, as an Englishman can, that my country has enjoyed constitutional freedom for centuries, and that the system is based on individual freedom and on the institutions that protect and guarantee them. The left has always been a thorn in Blair's side, and mine, too.

With George W. Bush I've had a different sort of relationship. I always had a good relationship with Kissinger, and he once said to me, "You're going to get along with Bush." I remember when they were doing the Florida ballot recount, during the presidential elections that saw George W. Bush elected President, and his father was coincidentally in Spain. He was a real bundle of nerves because it was such a close election, and naturally he wanted his son to win. I finally met him, and that's when Kissinger's prediction was confirmed. That was before September 11th.

Bush's first European trip after being elected President was to Spain. It wasn't to Great Britain or to France or to Germany. He started his European tour in Madrid. His commitment to the fight against terrorism was total. This was still months before September 11th. The King and Queen of Spain were the first Heads of State to visit the US after the elections. Bush has always been particularly sensitive to the importance of Spanish and Hispanic culture in the US and in the world. He was Governor of Texas and he knows the US Hispanic community. And it was clear that the US Administration had to draw up some new policies with respect to Europe. But that aside, I realized the moment I met him that he was a very special person. He had to become the first leader of the whole world, and he had before him the task of changing things. Some politicians are capable of that and they chart a new and historic path in the world. They have to prove what they're made of, and be willing to take on weighty responsibilities. George W. Bush is one of those leaders.

I share his view that, especially in a changing world like the one we live in, you need a strong leader and a leadership based on rock-solid principles and values, someone who can commit to the whole country. There are a few Presidents, not many, who have managed to change the United States. Bush is one of them. Reagan was another, as was Kennedy. But it's not just because of September 11th. It's because he realized what it meant, and the measures that were required to deal with it, and he knew how to respond to the American people. Of course, in Europe that's hard to understand. It's almost taboo. When I'm joking with him, I tell him that he's got an even worse reputation than Reagan in Europe, and that's worth bragging about. Don't forget that Reagan was central to the collapse of the Soviet Union.

George W. Bush and I have a close, personal relationship that he demonstrated on my last trip to Washington, in January 2004, with a farewell and a show of affection that go far beyond a mere political relationship.

The Iraq War and Spanish Public Opinion

The governments that I've presided over have always been pro-European, in favor of integration and of a united Europe. We've never, on the other hand, been in favor of the US taking unilateral action or of the Americans closing themselves off from the rest of the world. I don't believe that the US favors destroying European unity. I do believe that we have to open up and strengthen the European Union.

There's always someone ready to take on the privilege of defining what is European and, based on that, define who's in favor of Europe and who's against it, but that's another issue. For example, when we signed the so-called Letter of Eight about intervention in Iraq on January 30, 2003, *The Wall Street Journal* asked me to write an article about it. It had struck me that, instead of just me signing it alone, all of the European leaders who were open to US collaboration and the Atlantic link should sign. That's why I got in touch with Blair and we ended up publishing an article signed by eight Prime Ministers and national leaders: the two of us, as well as the leaders of Italy, Portugal, Denmark, Hungary, Poland and the Czech Republic. When the letter was first published there were eight of us and there ended up being eighteen.

This declaration was inevitably related to something that had occurred shortly before, when the anniversary of the Treaty of Versailles was celebrated and no other European countries were invited; this generated a feeling of exclusion and later defined France and Germany in their anti-intervention in Iraq position, which they claimed was the European position. Faced with that, Spain and the rest of the European member states had to decide if we had a position or not, if we accepted what France and Germany said or if we were going to adopt a common position to express our views. Well, that's what we did. That's what I explained in my article in *The Wall Street Journal*, which conveyed an important change, even a fundamental change, in recent history.

In the period before the Iraq intervention, I collaborated with the opposition the same way I had with the Socialists during the first Gulf War and the intervention in former Yugoslavia. I called José Luis Rodríguez Zapatero and told him that in 1990, when Iraq invaded Kuwait, I was leader of the opposition and I went to the Moncloa Palace in the same role he now had. I wanted a government policy not because it was my turn to govern but because then, as in 2003, Spain had to respond to a crisis situation as a unified nation. Now it was time for the PSOE to do the same from the opposition. I explained my reasoning for the decisions we'd made, which are the ones I've already laid out. I said I had nothing against including all the nuances and even the reservations he saw fit in the parliamentary debate, but that on a matter like this the government and the opposition had to be on the same side.

That's where the problems arose. Rodríguez Zapatero refused to accept that position and that was when the PSOE, the United Left and all their cohorts broke with the consensus that had always existed as far as Spanish foreign policy was concerned. This was something entirely new.

I'm convinced that it caused us to move backwards. Part of the Spanish left is entirely incomparable to the left in other countries. Deep down, the Spanish left still feels that everyone else, anyone who doesn't share their views, is unfit to rule. That's what we saw re-enacted in the campaign against the government's position on Iraq. It's the same thing they did to Antonio Maura in 1909 with the famous, "Maura, no." Personal factors are very important in politics. A lot of people thought I wouldn't step down after eight years in power. So just in case, they thought, we'll do everything we can to make sure the government has a hard time.

Here, in contrast with what happened in other European countries, they questioned a democratically elected government's legitimacy to rule the country. This wasn't a discrepancy over one point or even several. This was something more.

Obviously, the opinions people expressed were as legitimate as ours, whether they were broadcast by the media or shouted on the streets. But what they were expressing at demonstrations had to be translated into political action, and that's where things fell apart.

The opposition couldn't find a viable way to express their disagreement, so they went from a legitimate opinion to something that should never be done, which is to question the legitimacy of a democratically elected government. That's what kept them, for the most part, from being able to translate the demonstrations in early 2003 into a win at the polls. The opposition didn't offer a valid alternative and when the time came to stand before the voters, they had nothing to offer.

On top of that, there were several acts of violence. Every day there were attacks on Popular Party headquarters, and personal assaults on party members and members of the government. It was a mixture of aggression and pressure from the streets, and the country showed a very ugly, aggressive side, one capable of questioning the most basic things, questions of principle. And the opposition didn't condemn it as resolutely as they should have.

Dialogue is impossible in that kind of climate. All you can do is give in or carry on. If we'd caved in then, some of the basics of democracy in Spain would have come tumbling down and our institutional stability would have been jeopardized. It's one thing to lose the elections democratically, but it's quite another to allow your institutions to bow to the pressure. That's not democracy, but that was the chance we had to take. I was perfectly aware of that, but I never for a moment doubted what the right course of action was.

Leadership is forged in periods of calm, but it's proven in times of crisis. I had the legal authority bestowed upon me by the polls and there was absolutely no way I was going to change a policy I saw as just, legitimate and favored by a democratic majority. If we passed that test, it would be proof of Spain's democratic maturity. There would be no way to overthrow governments because of public demonstrations and pressure from the streets. Elections and the democratic system are vital.

I had the support of the government and of the Popular Party. I was sure that the Popular Party would rise to the challenge. But the pressure was so strong that I had reason to wonder how long people could withstand it. I was comforted to see that so many years of hard work were bearing fruit. It showed an expression of respect and of confidence in me personally, because there were indoubtedly a lot of people who weren't entirely convinced about all of our decisions, but in times of need they showed us that they trusted our reasoning and would accept our decisions.

This all culminated in the secret vote in the Congress of Deputies, the lower house of Parliament. There was an attempt to split the party but it became clear that the Popular Party wouldn't be split, that it's tough enough to withstand pressure and aggression. There wasn't a single Popular Group vote against the government. That's when the Popular Party showed what it's made of, showed that it was up to the historic responsibility of the moment and knew what had to be done. That frustrated the left even more.

You can't say the same is true of the opposition. Those days, anything went, as long as it was against the government, and they used everything they could to try to take make political gains from the situation. I was very surprised by the Catalan Convergencia i Unió party line. I had a lot of conversations with Jordi Pujol during that time, and I knew how he felt about the situation. So I was very surprised by the difference between what I knew his opinion to be and what his party was saying.

The Prejudices of the Left

Like almost everyone of my generation, I learned French in school and am a Francophone. I admired French culture, and even politics, as a model, as did many generations of Spaniards. France, too, is one of Spain's most important allies in many matters. They're our biggest trade partners, important investors and a critical export market for Spain. We've shared a lot throughout the course of history, as can be seen by the French influence in our country, and we'll keep sharing a lot more in the future.

However, regardless of having grown up in a climate where French influence predominated, I also admired Anglo-Saxon culture from a very young age. What I like about Anglo-Saxon countries is that they're serious countries, articulate countries capable of guaranteeing continuity, and that's fundamental. Their institutions are solid and have been maintained for long periods of time. They're also countries that know how to defend themselves and respond to aggression. Countries are strong when their institutions are strong and solid. That's one of the main objectives of any political action. Leaders have to make an effort to strengthen their institutions, to avoid succumbing to unnecessary tension, and to ensure that they never use their institutions for their own gain. This is especially true in Spain, where our institutions are still recent.

In that respect, what matters isn't public image or your oratory skills. I've never used my speeches as a tool to inspire admiration or enthusiasm. What you have to do is take a conviction, a plan, and turn it into a reality. That's the best way to teach by example. But it takes time, a lot of time, because it's not enough to just say things. You have to work so they become part of people's habits, part of the normal functioning of things, and part of politics.

It's true that on this point I've had to confront a very strong prejudice or different way of seeing things, as have many others. There was a strong French cultural component to my education but that never led me to draw the same conclusions that many of my generation did. What I mean is that I was never a socialist, never a "progressive", if you understand progressive to be the post-modern socialist guise. I've never believed in social engineering and I've never believed that the state could impose certain things on anyone, like their chosen path, the way they should live or the life plans they should make. Institutions are aimed at guaranteeing freedom within the law, not at imposing certain criteria or specific life patterns. I've never been a nationalist either. I have no complex about that, and I have no accounts to settle with the left or with the nationalists. I'm not embarrassed to be Spanish nor am I embarrassed about the history of Spain. There are some shady areas, some complications, but that's true of everywhere. Especially of important countries with long histories.

In September 2003, during a trip to the United States, I had to explain to the Cubans in Miami – not for the first time – that in Europe there are a lot of people who have just realized, after the June 2003 executions, that Fidel Castro is a dictator and his regime is an expression of pure totalitarianism. Until those people realized that things were not as they wanted them to be, there was no way to initiate change. But History proved we were right, as it had before. The definitive proof came with the fall of the Berlin Wall.

It's true that those people, a great deal of the members of my generation, had no choice but to come to more moderate, less dogmatic stances. In fact, many of them have abandoned their old, purely ideological, leftist outlooks. More than one probably votes Popular Party these days. But I thought it was pointless to try to change their beliefs. When the Popular Party came to power in 1996, they thought we were a parenthesis in Spanish history. Not just for reasons of immediate power or because they wanted to oust us as quickly as possible.

It was because in Spain, the left's great excuse was that we did-n't have the historical legitimacy needed to rule the country. That the Spanish center-right had gotten into power by accident or by some fluke. They tried to intimidate us with that. But it wasn't a tactical maneuver or a purely cynical move; it was also the illustration of a deeply rooted prejudice held by many people. And you can't reason against that type of prejudice; you can't persuade people rationally. The only thing you can do is teach by example, and that's a long-term project.

I've always believed in common sense, though. People under-stand, even if it's from their own personal perspective, that some things you don't do for ideological reasons or because you're following some hidden agenda. Some things you do because they're just common sense. For example, there have been a lot of arguments over education these past few years. In some instances there have been real battles. But a lot of what we were proposing was sheer common sense. Things like it being necessary to respect a teacher's authority in the classroom, or that students should have to prove they've learned something before advancing from one grade to the next.

In these cases I've always seen things so clearly that I thought everyone, or at least most people, would agree. These days, for example, there is no argument over the importance of a balanced budget in Spain. Everyone seems to agree on it. And nobody seems to want to raise taxes, either. So things end up taking shape.

But as far as Iraq goes, this wasn't the case. Something different, and much worse, happened. Iraq proved that sometimes the left's prejudice is more than just that, because when the left runs out of arguments, they don't always consider reality or think about their own attitudes. In fact, instead of trying to understand what happened, they decided to feed the negative response to the measures taken, the measures that have been proven justified, viable and sensible. That's when you end up with the kind of situation we had in Spain over the Iraq War. But little by little the Spanish public changed and began to look at things differently. That's where the Popular Party's strength comes into play, and where we see why the Socialists are unable to articulate any coherent opposition.

The Atlantic Link

Our relationship with the United States is advantageous in several respects. The US today guarantees security throughout the world. There is no alternative to that guarantee. Playing at drawing up other standpoints is frivolous, for Spain and for Europe. If security is guaranteed, so are the basic principles that uphold that security: the freedoms that democracy provides. They go hand in hand. Security is based on the establishment and the stability of open societies and democratic regimes. The world would be a much more dangerous place if we didn't have a good relationship with the United States.

Because of our geographic position and our ties to America, our interest in Atlantic politics is obvious. How can you explain Spanish history without America? We're also in NATO. From a Spanish perspective, not making the most of that Atlantic position would be a grave error of historic dimensions. And strategically, the biggest security issues in Spain indicate that we should nurture our relationship and contribute to its strength and permanence. I hope we do, regardless of who's in power in either Spain or the US.

This should all be compatible with Spain's European commitment. The way I see it, our friendship with the United States and our commitment to Europe have no reason to be incompatible. The facts and our day-to-day collaboration bear this out more than any temporary tensions that might arise.

I was sure, however, that the strategic differences between Europe and the United States were more complicated than they seemed, and had been so for some time. There were different perspectives, different interests and different traditions. The fall of the Berlin Wall and the September 11th attacks were interpreted differently in Europe and the United States. After the fall of the Berlin Wall a lot of Europeans almost thought that there were no more threats, that there was no longer any reason to keep preparing to guarantee security, since they thought it had already been achieved. And many Europeans, too, still thought in Cold War terms, imagining two opposing armies confronting one another, with a clearly demarcated boundary between the two, and a clear idea of the degree of threat each of them posed to the other. Things aren't like that anymore.

In fact, there is a new dimension to the situation. A lot of other countries now help guarantee world security; it's no longer just the United States and England. Spain is taking part in the reconstruction effort in Iraq and in security keeping, too, alongside Central American forces. This is the first time our troops have worked side by side outside of Latin America with Latin American troops. They are all magnificent soldiers. Latin America is joining the security defense apparatus, taking on responsibilities, and Spain is right there, by their side. This is part of the new dimension of the whole security issue. We have to help Latin America join the Atlantic link.

We've also worked with Polish troops. When I see a picture of Spanish troops and Polish troops together, it makes me think we're doing the right thing. In 1998 I called for a strategic alliance between Spain and Poland. I thought – and still think – that a good relationship between Spain and Poland is fundamental for many reasons, including the fact that we are similar countries with about the same number of inhabitants, and we are both interested in maintaining and reinforcing our Atlantic commitment. We also have certain cultural traits in common, and that makes it easier for us to understand one another. And then, of course, there is Poland's steadfast determination to remain independent, after having been mistreated so often through the course of their history. No one has ever given the Poles anything for free. And that gives them special courage.

When talk of enlarging the European Union began, people said we were against it. There was a campaign to try to cause a rift between our two countries, even though we had nothing against them. In fact the opposite is true; we became friendly and forged a strategic alliance even before the Iraq War. I myself signed it in 1998. We wanted Poland to become a great country, an emerging power.

Spain and Poland, along with other countries, have a lot to offer Europe. We can be a dynamic force socially, economically, and politically. The Poles, like many of the old Eastern bloc countries, are particularly receptive to less interventionist political action. They know what real state intervention is, and they know they don't want to go through that again. And for obvious historical reasons, but also because of their geographic situation, they are especially receptive to Atlantic politics. To them, the Atlantic link is the best guarantee of freedom and security. That's what they can offer classic European countries, the Europe that's always been protected by the Western bloc. To a large extent, that's also what we can offer.

We have to make sure Spain becomes one of the most important democracies in Europe. If we stay the course, we can do it by the end of the decade. My political duty is to lead the way, and my political desire is to keep us from straying. I am sincerely convinced that if we don't stray, we can achieve this. But that also means not just sitting tight. It means taking initiatives and having the ability to maintain them and to uphold our own position, too. It's true that when Spain kept quiet, when we had no criteria and let others chart our way it was easier, more comfortable. But that's not the Spain that I want, and it's not the Spain that I think my country deserves. I want Spain to be on the move; I want it to have its own voice and criteria. Even if sometimes people don't like it.

Parsley Island

With regard to the Parsley Island incident we did what we had to do, nothing more, nothing less. As soon as we found out that the Moroccans had taken position on the island we spoke to the Moroccan government and explained our view on the matter. Parsley Island had never had and should never have a military presence. That was always our stance. Then we sought support from Parliament, the European Union and NATO. But we had already resolved to intervene if necessary. I gave orders to prepare for a possible invasion, but I also said that I'd be the one to decide when the moment had come. We couldn't act until we were fully prepared and we'd gotten the necessary backing.

That's something that still differentiates us from other countries. After the Moroccan army occupied the island it took us a week to intervene, when other important countries would have done it the same day, in less than twenty-four hours. I said as much to several European Union colleagues. "I had to wait a week to do what you would have done in a day." It's a small yet symbolic difference. I hope nothing like that ever happens again, but if it does, I sincerely hope that whoever has to make the decision can do so immediately without having to wait for support, because they should already have that support.

We managed to get backing in very little time. The United States backed us, too. It wasn't as if we'd have called the US to ask for help or permission - nothing of the sort. But the US had their eye on the ball and they knew what was at stake. All the European countries realized, too, and almost all of them supported us, although there were some significant differences as to the degree of support, which were righted over time.

Morocco's occupation of Parsley Island was a serious challenge and it was also an ill-conceived challenge because it put the Spanish government in a position where we had no choice but to do what we did. That's why the public reacted the way they did. There were no demonstrations, no fervent outcries of any kind, the government always felt the people's support. I think Spaniards realized from the start that the government was doing what it had to do. And people were proud of the way we handled it, openly, sincerely, without making a song and dance of it. And things turned out well. I think we were right to make it clear from the start that we didn't want any trouble, that we had nothing to prove, that all we wanted was for things to go back to the way they had been before the Moroccan invasion. And that's what happened.

In 1991 Spain and Morocco signed the Cooperation and Friendship Treaty. King Mohammed VI paid us a visit in September 2001, and I had traveled to Morocco shortly before that. Morocco is the number one recipient of Spanish development funds and official aid. It's a country that Spanish companies have invested in heavily, and that's helped promote a new model for production that calls for a modern society and stable institutions in order to be fully developed. Morocco stepped up to that challenge years ago. And they've made extraordinary efforts and great strides towards the progress and well-being of their people, the stability of the Mediterranean and, clearly, towards Spanish national security.

That's why I was so worried. I didn't want any misunderstandings, and hoped fervently that our relationship with Morocco would proceed normally after the incident. Some said that since we'd intervened, we had to stay. That just wasn't the case. I am convinced that that's not what Spanish public opinion called for. But Spaniards felt that every time someone tried to push us around, we stepped back, lost ground. They were waiting to see if it would happen again, knowing – as I knew – that if it did, it would seriously hurt us. Spain couldn't be passive, sit tight after an aggression, especially considering other occasions when we'd failed to stand up and defend ourselves. And if we hadn't intervened, I'm sure things would have gotten much more complicated, not just for us but for the rest of Europe as well.

A Commitment to Defense

One of the most important decisions we've made with regards to national defense was the decision to abolish compulsory military service. It's remarkable, to say the least, that this was a decision that came from the center-right. It had been a long-running debate and there were still some who claimed that national defense would be threatened without compulsory military service. In actual fact, history shows almost the opposite to be the case. Conscription came out of the French Revolution. Spain's best armies were voluntary. And we had serious problems with our armies when they were not voluntary, even if that wasn't the reason why. I didn't want the army to be ornamental or symbolic. I had a different understanding of what the Armed Forces should be.

The first thing we had to do was to ensure that we had enough forces to defend the country. We had to adjust the size of the army to our real needs. Then Spain had to join NATO on equal footing, that is, join militarily and adjust our forces and resources to their demands.

Well, that's what we've been doing and our army has proven itself to be professional and efficient in joint efforts. The third issue was that if we wanted to take on responsibilities we had to improve our capabilities. There had been years of cutbacks, some of which actually halved the military budget – something unthinkable now – and years of continual asset stripping. We tried to change that. In 2003 we came out with some defense capabilities programs that had been a long time in the making; over the next several years, these will improve our defense situation. We are now contributing more to our military than anyone since Charles III.

Our efforts are aimed at making Spain capable of ensuring its own security and readying our army to take on the country's new responsibilities efficiently. Two Defense Ministers have been working towards this. Eduardo Serra oversaw the Spanish participation in the Kosovo War, professionalized the Armed Forces and demonstrated the importance we place on the continuity of certain policies by his presence. Serra is now President of the Royal Elcan Institute, a foundation that has managed to garner considerable prestige for its international policy studies and research on Spain's new global position in a very short time. Then Federico Trillo, who had been a chief parliamentary advisor to the Popular Group as well as President of the Chamber of Deputies, took on the task of modernizing the Armed Forces. His success in reforming the National Intelligence Center and overseeing Spanish military involvement – alongside our allies – in Iraq after the September 11th crisis has been exemplary.

In the Nineties, peacekeeping missions were the backbone of European foreign military intervention. And they'll still have their place in the future, but today we know that we're not safe from new threats. Spanish public opinion has to come to understand that this is vital. Without commitment nothing can be done, and an active commitment to defense is what guarantees a country's security. Without competent armed forces there is no foreign policy. That requires a lot of energy and a lot of effort. Soon after comes the feeling of satisfaction when things like what's happened recently occur and we have good, well-trained professionals ready to confront the situation and the resources necessary to fulfill their mission.

But in order for that to happen the military has to know that the public respects them and is willing to sacrifice so that they can do their jobs. It is absolutely vital that the public remember that soldiers are willing to put their lives on the line for their country and their fellow citizens. So in a few years, Spain will be able to have the kind of army it deserves, the kind of army befitting their role in the today's world.

A New International Outlook

The new threats that I've already talked about - terrorism, arms proliferation, and rogue states - require global solutions. We can provide political reliability and gravity. We're a stable country with strong, respected institutions. We can also contribute by offering military support, both in the form of troops and supplies, and with specials corps who are respected throughout the world. We're also important strategically, given our position in Europe and our relationship with Arab nations, which we have maintained throughout the years, including during the Iraq War.

The key to all this is convincing people that this is the way things really are. If you are of the mind that we should sit back and wait for another attack and take defensive action after it occurs, then we'll never get anything done. International law has to keep this fact in mind. Unless of course people actually think we have no right to defend ourselves, even knowing the nature of the new threats we're facing. You can't tell a country to sit tight knowing that others are planning to attack it, to try to make it weak. Those are the rules of the modern world.

The same goes for the terrorist threat in Spain. We have to be ready to take on our responsibilities. If we're not convinced of that or not willing to keep up our commitment fully then we can't ask anybody else to cover for us. The first thing they'll ask us is if we're willing to take the necessary measures to ensure our own security. If we don't do that, we can't ask anyone else for help.

That's why national awareness is so important. Without it, nobody will commit to defense and security. And our determination to work abroad, far from home, is borne of that awareness, because countries don't only defend themselves from within their own borders. They also defend themselves in distant lands, wherever new dangers arise.

We're not defending the United States in Iraq. We're defending an ally, but we're also defending Western democracy, and especially Spanish democracy. That, to a large degree, explains our conduct. What we're doing there is not substituting one dictatorship for another, one tyrant for another who suits us better. That's what the Soviet Union did when they extended their power and installed totalitarian dictatorships in the countries they conquered.

The United States isn't imperialistic. We don't have to share all of their objectives and every course of action they take, but you can't accuse them of having imperial designs. In fact, with the United States and other allied nations we are making it possible for Iraqis to live decent, dignified lives in a free, democratic regime. It's not easy, I know. Sometimes it seems impossible. But that's the only thing that lets *us* keep living in democracy. We're no longer living in a closed, isolated world. Threats no longer come from dictatorial regimes like the Soviet Union and the old Eastern bloc countries. Those countries followed the logic of non-aggression. They knew they depended on certain things to ensure their own security. But things aren't like that anymore. We're now facing threats that know no bounds, follow no rules, have no clear structures, no stable armies, and are supported by countries with no institutions to guarantee stability, transparency and public participation in political decisions.

That's why freedom at home has to be defended by helping develop stable democracies abroad. We're trying to spread democracy. That has to be Spain's position. Especially when we're talking about places where a good part of the fate of the world is at stake, as is the case in the Middle East and Iraq. If the Iraq operation is successful, if we can get them to build a stable regime, we will have made great strides towards solving problems in the entire region. We will have helped people there live better lives, and I'm not just talking about Iraqis, I'm also talking about Palestinians. But we'll also have taken a decisive step towards ensuring our own security and the stability of our system.

If things were to go poorly in Iraq, if we couldn't build a stable regime that guaranteed people there a dignified life, then we'd all have failed, especially in Europe. The United States would lose, too, but Europeans would lose more, because we're weaker to begin with, and we're closer to the conflict. If Turkey joins the European Union, we'll border Iraq. And if the attempt to stabilize Iraq fails and the United States takes a backseat in stabilizing the region, we're going to have a powder keg on our doorstep. It'll be our problem and we won't be able to ask the US to lend a hand when we haven't seriously tried to help them. That strikes me as critical. The longer we take in making decisions to commit our support to the project, the harder it will be to get started and to guarantee freedom and ensure security in the region and, eventually, in our own countries.

We can't fail. This is what happened in the Balkans. You could argue, then, that Spain had no direct interest in the Balkans. What did we have to do with it? But still, we helped overthrow Milosevic and stop the atrocities that were being committed. And that didn't seem to go down badly in the public's eyes.

So I have to wonder. What difference is there between our intervention in former Yugoslavia and the Iraqi intervention? Because UN Resolution 1443 supported the Iraqi intervention, and in the Balkans there was no such resolution. So the only difference is that during the Balkan War the Socialists were in power. And now, the Popular Party is in power. That's the difference.

Now the conflict in former Yugoslavia brought another problem to light, something closely related to terrorism. That was the presence of ethnic nationalism, which tends to lead to terrorism, in countries where it exists as well as abroad. In the case of former Yugoslavia, the atrocities were actually occurring in Europe. And yet it was Clinton who took action. Why? Because Europe had no real influence in the Balkans and couldn't change the course of events or put an end to Milosevic's brutal regime.

The US had to take charge in order to stop that bloodbath. And we helped the US. First the Socialists and then the Popular Party. We put no obstacles in the Socialists' path and supported their decision to back US intervention. In fact we agreed that it was part of a strong, consistent foreign policy that supported security and defended human rights. That's why we supported the government when we were in opposition. And that's why I at times thought that although the Socialists might not support our position on Iraq, they could have registered their dissent in a way that didn't disrespect our institutions.

The Iraq War, which is a consequence of September 11th, marked a decisive change in international relations. New threats, and the new alliances needed to stand up to them, require flexibility when it comes to decision-making and a much stronger commitment than previously necessary. They will also require a new conception of the institutions that allow those decisions to be made, such as the United Nations. The UN guarantees that international law is followed. It is absolutely vital that the UN backs the fight against international terrorism and helps build a safer, more democratic world.

Now, if the UN really wants international law to be respected it will have to consider how the global situation has changed. In the final analysis, the decisions made by the UN Security Council are constrained by the veto powers of the five permanent members: France, China, the United States, Russia and Great Britain. Now I'm not going to say we should restructure the UN. But it does seem obvious to me that we need to sit back and think about who's making those decisions and how they're being made. Especially because the complexity of the decision-making process subject to veto by any of the five countries contrasts enormously with terrorists' actions and the countries that support them. The UN is a very complex political and bureaucratic mechanism, but the same can't be said of terrorists who are poised and ready to strike at any moment.

Kofi Annan, UN Secretary, knows that. I've always had a very good, very respectful relationship with him, although we've disagreed on certain matters. But Kofi Annan is very aware of the changes that have occurred and he knows that reforms need to be introduced to strengthen the system of guarantees that the UN provides. And while they're getting underway, we can't stray from the path and lose our commitment to the fight against terror, which is why we have to be flexible and not obstruct international institutions. Clearly, we can't just go around pretending the world is a black and white movie, with the US and whoever supports them acting as the standard bearers for the Evil Empire and those who seek UN protection as the benefactors of humanity.

NATO is also a fundamental organization. NATO is the only source of stability in US-European relations. It's not that US-European relations are solely, or even mainly, upheld up by NATO, it's that NATO is the basic, fundamental instrument that guarantees them. We have to increase European defense capabilities; we have to be able to take on more powers and a bigger role. We must go beyond a simple commitment to humanitarian intervention and understand that in Europe we have common strategic and security interests. This has all finally started to manifest itself in increased military budgets and military spending in Europe. We've always been willing to help lay out a common European defense policy.

However, building up European defense should also be compatible with NATO rather than try to compete with it or substitute it. We don't have that kind of capacity, as the Balkan War proved. A lot of people who criticize NATO wouldn't be willing to absorb the cost that building up European defenses would entail in terms of human resources, materials and technology. Deep down, when people demand European security as opposed to NATO, what they're really demanding is that Europe stop taking responsibility for its own defense. It's as if they were saying to NATO – and in large part to the US – that they should take charge of defending Europe, and Europe, rather than working to defend itself, will stand around and criticize their every move and tell them how to do it.

If NATO were to be abolished, it wouldn't just be a multinational organization that could be replaced by another one. If NATO is abolished, then the Atlantic link is broken, and that's what Western security and stability depend on, especially European countries. Europe should build up its defenses in order to strengthen the Atlantic link. We've made important efforts here. By joining NATO's military apparatus we've endorsed a course of action that supports European defense, we've committed to an Atlantic perspective and we've made efforts to take part in joint military operations.

There are Spanish troops in Bosnia-Herzegovina, in Kosovo, in Afghanistan, in Abu Dhabi and in some African countries, like Ethiopia. In October 2003 there were 1,412 Spanish soldiers in Iraq. On the same date, there were 3,731 Spaniards on peacekeeping missions around the world. Other countries are following our army's reconstruction with interest. That's the best signal we can give to show that we take this matter seriously and we're committed to joint defense.

But if someone were to say to me that our efforts should be aimed at bringing down NATO, I would say no. No way. In Parliament the opposition often talked about European defense and the need to take measures to strengthen European defense. I never asked what they wanted that European defense for; I don't think I would have liked the answer. But if you want to spend you also have to consider where the funds are going to come from, and what other expenses you're willing to sacrifice to build up that defense.

It's important to know why defense needs to be invested in. Spaniards have to understand that their freedom depends on Spain's influence in the world, and that that influence will be inexistent without a reasonably equipped army, one that's up to the task of defending human rights and the principles of legality that uphold democracy. That's what matters. The determination and the capability to defend Western values, which are the values I believe in.

CHAPTER SIX

In the Vanguard of Europe

I've been through some very tough negotiations in the European Union, the first of which was at the European Council meeting in Amsterdam, in 1997. That was when we were discussing the relative weight of each country in terms of decision-making powers and European institutions. At about midnight, Wim Kok, the Dutch Prime Minister, announced that, if everyone present was in agreement, he was going to conclude the session. That's when I set out our position: because of our size, geographic position, and historic and economic circumstances, Spain, I said, is in a special situation. And that means we have to keep negotiating the terms of the agreement.

That started a very lively discussion. I went out with Helmut Köhl, the German Chancellor, and we locked ourselves in a room, determined to solve the problem. There were a lot of people against us. Tony Blair was there and he lent a hand with negotiations for a while. And three hours later, at about 4:00am, we came up with a formula that would work. It was a declaration that recognized Spain's unique circumstances, which was crucial in helping us with the Treaty of Nice negotiations later. That was when they modified the European institutional decision-making mechanisms to correspond to a more realistic vision of Europe, with twenty-five member states.

The other particularly tough negotiations were over what came to be known as Agenda 2000. It contained several points, including the approval of a new economic framework for 2000-2006 aimed at dealing with the Union's new challenges, such as expansion. We had already negotiated aid to Spain within the Common Agricultural Policy framework; that financial assistance was, and still is, absolutely essential to our agriculture and livestock industries. And although Loyola de Palacio had managed not only to secure the aid but also increase it, I said we shouldn't cry victory yet, because we still had Agenda 2000 in front of us, and that was going to be even tougher. The negotiations took place in Berlin in 1999, and we were given a very simple choice: here are the cuts, take it or leave it. That's what they told us. Well, obviously, if that was going to be their approach, and if their approach hurt Spain, I said I'd leave it.

Then various people started telling me that Spain was standing alone, that no one backed my position. And indeed I did feel like I was standing alone, but I was also convinced that I had to stand firm and that there were other countries in a very similar position. And though I was sorry to have to do that, the terms they offered were simply not reasonable terms; it was no way to reach an agreement. So we started another round of negotiations that night and went on into the small hours. I remember I gave a press conference at 6:00 or 7:00am. It was a great success. Financially, Spain had never secured a better deal. Between 2000 and 2007, we'll have received more funding than we've ever received from the Union.

It's important to keep in mind that by this time the drive behind a certain course of action in building up the Union was gone. On the one hand the single market had already been established. But on the other, there was still the need to build the unity and solidarity so strongly backed by European heavyweights of the Eighties and Nineties like Helmut Köhl and Jacques Delors. The social cohesion fund was created in the early nineties, setting the mechanisms for internal cohesion in motion. By the late Nineties, the push for unity and solidarity had waned. The European Union had gone from twelve member states in 1986 to fifteen in 1996. In 1999 there were twenty-five on the horizon. So financial cutbacks were put in place. Where could they be made? In agriculture, which France objected to, and in social cohesion funds, which affected us.

Those were logical cutbacks, but they also had to consider our position. All the Socialists had done was ask Europe for more and more money, without making the effort required to actually use the funds to benefit the Spanish economy. Since we *were* making the effort with the economic policy measures we embarked on as soon as we reached power, we could and should ask the other member states to make the same effort. And that's what we achieved in Berlin in 1999.

We've seen the results; Spain has made significant advances. Prosperity has risen, far more people are employed and Spanish incomes are at 87% of average European incomes. Those are measures of real success, and now the time has come for us to work with the new members. But they're already making an effort, as well. In the European Union, member states pay a sum that depends on their GDP and on each country's VAT. We still receive aid because of our position vis-à-vis the European average, but we also contribute a lot more than we used to.

We have to be accepting of the countries that are now joining, but we also have to keep in mind that the cuts being put in place are not solely based on the Union's expansion. They want to make cutbacks categorically, regardless of the number of member states. That's something we need to negotiate in the future. But what we've negotiated so far was a great success for Spain. A success that some people still hold against me.

Our Contribution to Europe

My first European Council meeting was in Florence in 1996. As I said, abolishing existing European extradition procedures for terrorist crimes was the first thing I put on the table. We argued our point, a lot of people were opposed, and it didn't get any further than that at the time. Then came an informal meeting in Austria, when Viktor Klima, a Social Democrat, was Chancellor. Klima allocated tasks and suggested I develop the point on security and counter-terrorist policy. It was then further outlined and laid out at the Tampere European

Council meeting, when the Common Space of Freedom, Security and Justice was agreed upon. When Spain occupied the Presidency of the European Union we improved it further, as everyone recognized. After the Tampere meeting, whenever Paavo Liponen, Prime Minister of Finland, had to talk about those matters, he'd say, "That's José María's subject."

We consider it a fundamental part of our contribution *to* the European Union, but also beyond it. We helped create Common Space of Freedom, Security and Justice. We helped introduce substantial changes to international law on terrorism and also supported international tribunals in the prosecution of human rights abuse cases. Some progress had already been made, of course. The Schengen Area had been created, committing member states to adopt common security measures. And work had been started on the creation of European citizenship. But there was still a lot to do and many of the things we were trying to set in motion met with serious resistance.

In terms of security measures, one date marks a turning point. That's September 11th. After September 11th, what we'd been aspiring for for years was suddenly achieved at great speed; resistance virtually disappeared. The change was dramatic. Of the fifteen member states, there had been nine that initially didn't even have terrorism classified as a crime. There were loopholes that allowed for talk about financing terrorist groups, there were terrorist groups that were considered political parties, and in some cases terrorist crimes didn't even carry sentences. A large part of Europe was hopelessly behind on these matters. They lived in a happy-go-lucky world that September 11th brought crashing down.

Because of our long battle against terror, we were relatively advanced on these matters. From that moment on, we became moral and political leaders in this sphere. That's nothing to be proud of, because it would be better to be able to say that we no longer had any terrorism in our country, but at least we can say we were up to the task and we put our experience at the service of European citizens' freedom and security.

We had superb partners in this undertaking, in the form of our three Foreign Affairs Ministers. Abel Matutes had a distinguished track record and experience in the European Commission, and the first NATO expansion - which incorporated Hungary, Poland and the Czech Republic - was negotiated under his mandate. Spain's third Presidency of the European Union went brilliantly thanks to the hard work of Josep Piqué. And Ana de Palacio brought with her direct European Union institutional experience. She had to face some tough times starting the very moment she came to the Ministry, and later during the Iraq conflict and the negotiations at the United Nations and with the rest of Europe, as well as with the Donors' Conference in Madrid. Ana de Palacio made an extraordinary political contribution with her tenacity and hard work; she did more than she's often given credit for.

We've always insisted that the European Union was more than a single market, that its foundations are not exclusively economic and that it's also a political union. Spain's commitment has always been very clear on this. There's not a single section, not a single point of European politics that we haven't participated in, and we've been front and center for much of it, offering proposals and initiatives. In terms of domestic market directives, Spain is one of the most open and advanced countries. In defense, we have members in every European defense decision-making body and have contributed to common defense in every way we can. We helped create the Common Space of Freedom, Security and Justice and turn it into the third pillar of the European Union.

However, there are many ideas about what the European political union should be, and I should say that I have never had a federalist conception of Europe. As far as I see it, the European Union is a union of states with common, integrated policies, but one that also includes inter-governmental cooperation and their own national policies, too. I see Europe as having nations and states. It's not some random conglomeration of people with no history and no identity. Ortega said that the idea of Europe predated the idea of European nations, and that's probably true; but he also said that nations are a fundamental part of Europe. There is no way to conceive of Europe or the European Union without the national framework, and definitely not *against* that framework. Quite the opposite, in fact. The stronger and more prosperous the member states are, the more dynamism and leadership ability the Union will have.

Building Up the Union and European Spirit

Another one of our difficult moments with regard to Europe took place during the European Council meeting in Nice in December 2000, when we reached an agreement on the construction of European institutions in the immediate run-up to the Union's enlargement. We were no longer talking about fifteen or even twenty-five members. In fact, there were twenty-five present at the Nice negotiations. The Nice Council meeting undertook institutional negotiations for twenty-seven countries. France raised the vital question of maintaining parity with Germany. In truth, we were all willing to recognize that Germany was in a better position. The Treaty of Nice marked the culmination of the institutional reforms that led to the Union's enlargement to begin with. Negotiations were complex, because decision-making with twenty-seven members is much harder than it is with fifteen, but we all seemed satisfied with the results. We'd reached a new balance in terms of decision-making powers, one that took into consideration the existence of large countries, small countries, and medium-sized countries like Spain.

The European Convention mandate, originally conceived as a meeting of distinguished political and academic minds, came out of Nice. It was charged with reexamining powers, simplifying treaties and drafting common policy. The aim was to draw up a text that would be more accessible to all Europeans.

However, the Convention had no mandate to carry out an institutional inspection. It was not supposed to repeal decisions that had been previously adopted, such as the Treaty that came out of the Nice Council. But that was exactly what it did. At the Nice European Council meeting we achieved a representational balance that considered big countries like France and Germany, small countries, which are numerous, and medium-sized countries such as Spain and Poland. Any changes to this accord could result in serious imbalances: big countries would pull more weight, small ones could end up being used as pawns, and intermediate ones would be left with no room to maneuver.

The European Union is a double union of states and of citizens. The citizens have a voice in Parliament through proportional representation. And the states, in turn, are represented in the European Council. But they tried to change the rules of the game and apply proportional representation to the states in the European Council.

This contradicts the spirit of the European Community's founding Treaty, the 1957 Treaty of Rome. It directly contradicts the spirit that led Europe to become a political unit and it denies the values that the entire Europe project has been based on until now. It does favor some countries, no doubt about that. But it doesn't favor the idea of the European Union and it doesn't favor Spain's national interests. These are important things to keep in mind when assessing the situation.

Speaking of values, I have always been strongly in favor of making reference to Christianity in the European Constitution. And I've found some allies in the new member states such as Poland on this.

Mentioning Christianity doesn't mean that Europe should be a Christian nations club. That's absurd. In fact, I've also been strongly in favor of allowing Turkey membership to the European Union. Turkey is a very strong, populous country with a proven track record of loyalty to Western values, military commitment to the defense of the West, and it's a strategically situated democracy that could set a very valuable example in terms of spreading freedom to parts of the world that are very close to us. I understand that not everyone agrees, but I see it as worthwhile to secure a country like Turkey, with a majority

Muslim population, in a space like the European Union that respects freedom and human rights.

However, just because the European Union isn't a Christian club doesn't mean we have to deny our roots. I'm not trying to forge a denominational European Union, nor do I think anyone else is. No one wants to question the laic principles of the European Constitution. But you can't deny the facts. The idea of Europe, the idea Ortega talked about that allowed for nations to be created, and then, in the mid-20th century, allowed for the creation of a common political and economic space, cannot be understood without reference to Christianity. There's the philosophical, artistic and intellectual legacy of Greece, the legal, institutional and political legacy of Rome, the political framework of freedom that began in the Middle Ages, and the critical and rationalist spirit of the Renaissance and the Enlightenment. And none of that can be understood without examining Christianity's contribution to our beliefs, norms and values. To put it any other way is to deny the facts before us.

The same is true of Spain. How can you explain Spanish history without Christianity? It wouldn't make any sense. The Visigoth Monarchy, the Reconquest of Spain from the Moors, the Catholic Monarchs, the Discovery of America and subsequent evangelization there…None of it, none of Spain's contribution to civilization makes any sense without a clear conception of Christian faith.

Now, of course, that bears no relation to whether or not we all share the same beliefs. Religion is, as far as I'm concerned, a purely individual matter, one that each person must resolve in his or her own free conscience. But you can't deduce, from that, that our cultures share no common roots.

I'm in favor of a political structure like ours, that is, a civil rather than denominational order, one where the state is obliged to respect religious freedom and where there is a place for all religions, one where religious practice is fundamentally seen as an individual freedom. But you can't deny that Europe is a civilization and all civilizations share a series of values whose ultimate foundation, at least as far as Europe is concerned, rests on Christianity. Denying Europe's Christian roots is more than denying a historic reality, it's denying the very foundations that uphold our individual and social outlook.

Every society has values, principles and beliefs on which the very existence of its people rests. If those are denied, as some would have us do in the case of the European Constitution, then there is no way for people to acquire the moral criteria necessary to make their own decisions. You end up landing nowhere.

That might seem attractive to some people. A cynical Europe that disregards the values that built it would no doubt be fun, even highly entertaining to some. But the risks are too great, because it would also be an insignificant Europe. When values have no historical sustenance, nothing is worthwhile, unless you just want to float along in prosperity. There is nothing worth fighting for, nothing worth defending.

If Europe falls into some sort of political hedonism, it will end up a society in decline rather than a dynamic, progressive society. As a result, political initiative and a political action will be enormously restricted, because there will never be enough reason to do anything, to commit to anything other than the prevailing public opinion of the day. Right now we're in the heyday of political correctness, which by the way can be as politically correct as it wants, but it was never a democratically elected option, it's just managed to set itself up as if it were. In the future, who knows what other options there might be and what other directions they might take. And in that moral insignificance lies the seed of totalitarianism.

Europeans have been through things like this before, not with the same social or historical characteristics, but we've seen moral principles dissolve on other occasions. And we know what the political consequences were. Díez de Corral spoke of Europe's abduction, when half the continent was just emerging from one type of totalitarianism and the other half was being subjected to another type.

A failure to define a common position means that Europe will have a tough time making the kinds of commitments to security, defense and political stability that it needs to make. That's one of the most serious problems - maybe the most serious problem - that we face in Atlantic politics right now.

New Challenges: Expansion and the Mediterranean

I always wanted Spain, in addition to receiving the support it deserves from the European Union due to its geographical situation, to contribute decisively to building the Union. Spain should do as much it can in its capacity as an increasingly prosperous country. We have to keep making decisive contributions, as we have until now, like liberalization policies, the single market, justice, security and defense. We also have to make an effort to ensure that the spirit of the Treaty of Rome is respected, as are the values that uphold European civilization, the birthplace of Western civilization.

But there are other challenges, too. For historical reasons Europe has until now had a particularly Western and Central European perspective. Now it's opened up to the countries that Pope John Paul II calls "Europe's second lung," countries that were always – even when they were in the Soviet sphere of influence – part of the trunk of the same tree of European civilization.

We support these countries' integration into the Union not just because it's in our national interests. For that to be true, we have to take advantage of the opportunities for investment and partnership they offer from the second they join. But besides that, there is also the Western dimension that these countries, having suffered totalitarianism first hand, bring to Europe. They know the value of freedom, they hold Western values dear and know how crucial our Atlantic relations are. We should pay close attention to what they do and even be prepared to learn from the signals they send us.

Spain is very uniquely placed, geographically, and that gives us great opportunities in the Mediterranean. There have been many interesting plans in this area, such as the Barcelona Process, but Europe's Mediterranean policy has always been incipient. This is due to both the complexity of the region and to the Union's need to deal with other pressing matters from within the continent.

Our relations with Morocco have sometimes been tenuous, but that's the way it tends to be with neighbors. We've increased the scope of our relationship with Algeria and established direct contact with Iran. I have visited Libya, a country whose increasing international-ization shows a great desire to return to normalcy. The King and Queen visited Syria on a trip that was a very important expression of our will to contribute to stability in the region. We're also committed to helping negotiate a solution to the Arab-Israeli conflict. These have been years of modest but continuous hard work towards drafting a policy. And now we have a little room for maneuver that's allowed us to make some difficult decisions, such as supporting intervention in Iraq, without jeopardizing our position or our relationships.

It's very important, not just for Spain but for Europe as a whole, that the Mediterranean and the Middle East achieve a level of stabili-ty, because they're our neighbors and because they should be able to become prosperous democracies. Borders are another issue. Turkey's joining the Union, for example, will mean that the European Union borders Iraq. That's very important, though we should also keep in mind that nowadays borders are really only important when it comes to creating and delimiting a country. In terms of security, borders are not what they used to be. With the new threats we face, security no longer means territorial defense. Now it's more about neutralizing and eliminating risk. And this is another of Spain's European contributions, through maintaining and expanding what I call an Atlantic Europe.

Latin America

The concept of an Atlantic Europe is similar to referring to Christianity in the European Constitution in the sense that it's impossible to understand Europe without it. The way that the European Union is set up is fundamentally connected to an Atlantic relationship. Does anyone really think Stalin would have stopped in Prague or Budapest otherwise? Some purportedly intelligent people like to speculate about an independent Europe, which would be the Europe that should act as a counterweight to some other power. It's absurd. The only Europe possible is the Atlantic Europe. Without the Atlantic guarantee there would be no Europe. That, the Atlantic Europe, is the real one, the one we know, the one we trade with and move through. Any conception of Europe that attempts to weaken or break our Atlantic link is, among other things, suicidal.

For Spaniards, the Atlantic affects us directly. Spain can't be understood without an Atlantic dimension. Without Latin America, without the Atlantic scope of politics and Spanish culture, we'd be an entirely different country. It's part of our identity, of our very nature.

Since I believe in the idea of the West, I also believe that we should include the American continent – all of it -- in the Atlantic world. That undertaking has been one of Spain's greatest contributions to Europe and to the West, and should continue to figure in our plans.

The Ibero-American Community of Nations is a reality that demands we make increasing efforts. We share projects, values and interests with these countries. We must keep strengthening our ties.

If we speak in cultural terms, we share a language with 400 million people and an extraordinarily energetic culture that has Spanish as its common bond, a varied, globalized culture that's expressed in Spanish, one that can compete with other cultures and serve as a platform for our initiatives.

It's critical that Latin America join in the task of instituting democracy and rebuilding countries that respect international law, as some countries did with their efforts in Iraq. And of course we're very interested in stability in Latin America itself.

The prospect of incidents that could weaken democracy in Latin America worries me greatly. Their democratic advances have been extremely important. And just as I think that populism is the worst formula – whether from the left or the right – I also think that what Latin America needs most are decisive politicians determined to reinforce institutional democracy. Spain has done what it can to cooperate and will continue to do so. But those are intermediate to long-term actions that should help underpin the huge changes that have taken place in a relatively short time. In this sense, what Lula da Silva is doing in Brazil is important, and so is the step Spain has taken by helping expand our common interests, as seen recently by the Spain-Brazil strategic agreement. That will be one more proof that there are alternatives to the populist temptation.

Cuba is still the exception to the positive outlook. I have avoided arguing with Fidel Castro, because every argument favors him. I've been insulted for suggesting that in Cuba, as in any other country in the world, respect for human rights should be a priority. I don't care. Just as I've never felt even a smidgen of admiration for Marxism, I've also never respected a regime that doesn't know what democracy is, or what legality and human rights are. But what I do care about are the Cuban people. I don't think the Castro regime will outlive the man. Meanwhile, we'll keep trying our best to help Cubans through our international commitments. But, knowing as we do that relations with Cuba are not just political but also sentimental and deeply emotional, my desire is to see Cuba become more like Spain.

We want Latin America to guarantee stability and security, and in part that's also because we want to defend our interests in the region. A few years ago we complained that we had no multinationals. Now we do. And where are they? To a large extent they're in Latin America. For example, we are Brazil's number two investor in the world. We're the top European investor in Latin America. So what happens in Latin America doesn't only affect Latin America, or even all of South and North America. It also affects us. Directly. That presence is part of Spain's new reality and we have to face up to it. We have to shoulder our responsibility, to realize the role we play in the world. We're no longer a country that depends on the interests and actions of others. We're self-reliant. We depend on our own decisions and on ourselves.

Europe's Sphere of Influence

A substantial part of Spain's political reality and scope lies in the Atlantic. That fact guarantees stability so it entails considerable advantages. It's also got its disadvantages and its risks. If we want to be an important country and keep prospering we have to be prepared to make certain decisions. Cambó used to say that if you try to create an oasis you end up losing everything that surrounds the oasis as well as the oasis itself. And that's just it: prosperity can't just depend on one country. So you have to cooperate with other countries if you want to be prosperous, and you have to provide safety if you want to be free.

The stronger Europe is economically, the stronger it will be politically. Unfortunately, Europe has lost its place in line over the past few years. In the Nineties, we fell drastically behind the United States. We've fallen behind in prosperity, dynamism, initiative and productivity. We now run the risk of continuing to increase the gap and losing out on even more opportunities.

That's why I'm insistent on our need to regain the growth potential and prosperity that I know Europeans are capable of. But in order to do so, we need economic reforms and we need to undertake initiatives that will put us back on the starting line. We have to put liberalization measures in place, become more flexible, establish a true single market, and open new doors.

Over the last twenty years, the European Union has been dragging its feet compared to the United States in terms of employment and growth. Some of us wanted to remedy this situation and we – Tony Blair helped especially on this – put out an economic initiative in March 2002 on what was known as the Lisbon Agenda. It was an attempt to make the European Union the most dynamic region in the world. Amongst other things, it advocated completing the domestic market and deregulating the financial sector, energy and the service sectors. Spain has advanced a lot in this direction but not everyone else has followed suit. The result is that Europe isn't growing as much as it should and won't be able to meet the Lisbon target of a 70% employment rate by

2010. If that's true, we'll keep losing opportunities to other countries and it will be impossible to compete with them.

Spain has followed a different course of action to some of our neighbors. We're experiencing higher growth rates, creating most of Europe's jobs (in 2003 90% of European employment was created in Spain) and we contribute a lot of money to many parts of the world. However, what's now happening in most of Europe is what used to be true of Spain with respect to the rest of Europe. Namely, they are not approaching convergence with the richest economies like the United States. So our sphere of influence doesn't increase. And if we don't exhibit economic growth, we'll lose the ability to influence the rest of the world.

I am convinced that we need to work towards the creation of a large, financial economic area that encompasses both the European Union and North America, and that we can do it by 2015. This large area should aim to include Latin America; that would indisputably increase stability and global prosperity. That's what I proposed on my last visit to Washington.

Some people say that's anti-European. I really don't understand that. Playing at decreasing our own prosperity, growth potential and stability is what's anti-European, if you ask me. Risking our Atlantic relationship for the sake of creating some supposed counterweight that gets us nowhere is anti-European. It's pointless, in a word.

Europe is capable of advancing towards greater prosperity and greater responsibility if we set out to do it. I'm not going to lecture anyone, but Spain kept up the Stability Pact under very difficult circumstances, and we did it in spite of the fact that the pact was an expression of distrust towards southern European countries and their ability to establish serious economic policies. We met the terms the countries that imposed the pact are not meeting. And it's not a matter of some meeting the terms and some not, because we all go through hard times. The problem is that it's stopped being an interim situation and turned into a serious, structural problem. Countries that achieve greater flexibility and make advances in reform will be the ones that generate more prosperity and more confidence. Those that don't undertake reforms, even if they're richer and more powerful today, will have a much harder time in the future.

They'll also make it harder for the rest of us. The economic and social reforms that the Lisbon Agenda advocated were distorted and neutralized. Then the Stability Pact was questioned, and this isn't just a matter of economic policy. This is about credibility and trust. And it doesn't only affect the countries that don't meet the terms, either. It affects the credibility of the institutions of the European Union, which is incapable of complying with the very terms it sets out, and it affects the rest of the Union's member states, because it comprises a dense framework of relations in which no single party is isolated.

What I can't understand is why we are reproached, in Spain, for defending the European Union and Spain's interests in the Union. It's perfectly legitimate for each country to defend its own interests in the Union. What's more, it would be incomprehensible for them not to. It's very hard to understand how *Spaniards* could reproach us for defending Spanish interests. I know that Germany carries a lot of weight because of its position, its population its prosperity and its sphere of influence. And I know perfectly well that Germany tries to marry its national interests with general European interests. But they aren't the only country to do it. We also propose measures and defend agreements that are in our vital interests and that are good for the European Union as a whole.

This attack on the defense of Spanish national interests ironically launched by some Spaniards is based on a false perception of Spanish reality. We received considerable help from Europe when we were a less developed country. Now we face another set of problems, which are not the same as the old ones. They are the problems faced by prosperous countries. But I'd rather a country face problems that result from prosperity than those that stem from poverty.

CHAPTER SEVEN
Fighting Terrorism

Right from the outset, the fight against terrorism was a government priority. The Popular Party had signed the Ajuria Enea Pact in 1988 and, naturally, we had kept our promise to support the previous government's counter-terrorism policy. However, we never agreed with the idea of making under-the-table agreements, known here as "temperature checks", or with undertaking talks, like the previous government had with terrorists.

Our strategy is based on four ideas. First and foremost, we are convinced that it is possible to end terrorism. For many years people went around espousing the belief that there is no solution to terrorism. That's just not true. The fight against terrorism will end, and it will end with the defeat of the terrorists.

Second, our approach is to wage open war on terrorism, standing strong and showing no mercy. We were convinced that that was fundamental, because it was the only way for terrorists to know we meant business. They had to know that we would hunt them down. Thirdly, we were determined to act within the rule of law, respecting all of the democratic rights provided by our system. And finally, we began a global offensive to increase international cooperation.

The war on terror was always a priority based on these four tenets. In Spain, most of the population supported us on this. Internationally that wasn't necessarily the case, though our relations with France had improved and, at least formally, there had always been a show of solidarity on their part. But in terms of legislation and a stance against terrorism, it was still generally considered a localized problem, something that affected a few countries, which deserved a show of solidarity, yes, but when it came down to it, they should sort out their own problems as best they could.

We weren't willing to let things carry on like that. We knew that terrorism wasn't just a localized problem and that it had to be tackled head on, taking its true scope, which extends far beyond national borders, into consideration. After September 11th the success with which our international offensive was met gathered tremendous speed.

Our Stand Against Terror

The Socialists' last years in power were difficult and problematic at the Ministry of the Interior. What happened made people lose faith in those in charge of the ministry, and there was only one way to remedy that: through deeds and political action. We had to get back to normal as soon as possible. Obviously, this meant that we had to act within the law. Counter-terrorist operations could not steamroller over democratic law.

Then we had to salvage certain counter-terrorist organizations that for one reason or another hadn't been used. When we came into office, the national police hadn't been involved in counter-terrorism operations for quite some time. We decided to change that, and that meant we had to change command, regain the confidence of the national police officers and equip them properly.

I decided to have Jaime Mayor Oreja head up the new policy as Minister of the Interior. In political terms as well as in terms of taking concrete action, he was the best man to develop and execute our plan. Jaime Mayor not only understood perfectly the logic behind the policy, he was coauthor of it. So there was no better man to translate it into action. I was sure of that then, and I was sure of it after the 2000 elections. It may not have been what he wanted, and I understand that, but it was crucial that he keep on in that capacity.

I need to point out two things with respect to our support for previous governments. We always backed the government's counter-terrorist policy. They always had our support, although, I also thought that maintaining contact with terrorists was a mistake. It didn't stop them from striking when they had to, of course, but it led to a state of confusion that did nothing to bring down either terrorism or those who support it.

In the late Seventies and early Eighties, terrorists had killed off the Basque Country UCD. Those were times of brutal, merciless terror. The terrorism was devastating and as a result, for a long time afterward, we had no institutional protection, no refuge in the Basque Country. Our party members were totally exposed; there was nowhere for them to take cover. That left us with two possibilities: let the party disappear or fight back. We were determined to develop the strong moral fiber that would guarantee the party's continuity.

Two things determined the Popular Party's survival in the Basque Country. The first is women. There were many women who stayed true and kept the party together throughout its toughest times. Without them, local headquarters would have had to close. The party's women kept them open, spoke, paid visits; they got things done, in short. That was vital. We'll never fully be able to express how grateful we are for their bravery, for what they did in conditions so terrible that, even today, they are hard to imagine.

Young people were the other thing that kept us afloat in the Basque Country. At some point, groups of young people began to come forward, people who realized that they had to make a stand against terror and violence and declare themselves in favor of cooperation and tolerance. And just as the women kept the party alive, the young people assured its future. Without those two groups, without their understanding of what was at risk, their making the sacrifice and proving that the Basque Country was still free, the Popular Party there might have gone under. We owe them a debt of gratitude that we'll never be able to repay.

We did everything we could from Madrid to support them and

comfort them to the highest possible degree. And people rise to the challenge if they see where the government is headed and see that their problem is an absolute government priority and will continue to be one for the long haul. But the government was only able to do what it did because its party members were steadfast and showed their ability to fight back, bravely and patriotically.

The Offensive Against the Popular Party

Before the 1996 elections, ETA tried to eliminate the alternative we were proposing with a full-on attack on the Popular Party. They were attempting to destroy our capacity to react, to do as much damage as possible, to kill any hope for change.

They launched their offensive on January 23, 1995, with the assassination of Gregorio Ordóñez. He was our man in San Sebastian. I knew him well. We had gotten together frequently and we had a very good relationship. In fact, we'd been together just two or three days before he was murdered. He had invited me up to San Sebastian, and I returned again for the annual Tamborrada Festival held there because he asked me to expressly. We wandered through the streets together and then went out for dinner. When we walked in, the whole place stared at us in silence. But when we left, a group of people applauded and showed us their support.

Gregorio Ordóñez was a remarkably brave and courageous man. He always said what he felt. He put on an incredibly brave face. Occasionally I would give him advice or make a suggestion, and sometimes you just had to let him do things his way because he had a very strong personality and any attempt to temper it meant diluting what was most valuable, his intensity, his bravery and his integrity. He'd just gotten married and had a baby, only a few months old.

When he was murdered I traveled up to the Basque Country, and in the hotel room I told Jaime Mayor Oreja that he should stand as Popular Party candidate in San Sebastian. He was the most prepared;

he knew our policy better than anyone. And besides, we owed it to Gregorio's memory. And he accepted the candidacy, showing the same discipline and loyalty that he's always shown.

After Gregorio Ordóñez was assassinated they tried to kill me, in April 1995. With that attempt they made it very clear that their intention was literally to kill off the alternative. They'd realized that we were after them. But that time things didn't work out for them. And it didn't change any of my views on how the war on terror should be fought.

When we came to power in 1996, our position was crystal clear. In terms of Basque nationalism and the PNV (Basque Nationalist Party), we had to embark on the road to political normalization and try to get rid of a whole series of prejudices that history had conferred on us. We didn't want any ambiguity or obsequiousness. We had to make it perfectly clear that we were open to the Basque Country, we had nothing against them, but that we were also very firm in our stance against terrorism.

Then there was a waiting period that lasted a few months. It was as if ETA just wanted to sit back and watch for a while, see what we'd do. But after that they unleashed a brutal campaign that ended on July 12, 1997 with the assassination of Miguel Ángel Blanco.

Miguel Ángel Blanco's murder was ETA's response to the Civil Guard freeing José Antonio Ortega Lara, who had been kidnapped and tortured for 532 days. Ortega Lara was freed on June 30, 1997 in one of the security forces' great successes. No one who saw him then could possibly forget Ortega Lara's face as he emerged from the underground hole where they'd kept him locked up for eighteen months. He looked like he'd been in a concentration camp. It was obvious that they were trying to starve him to death.

The brutality of Miguel Ángel Blanco's assassination, and the cruelty that Ortega Lara was subjected to were so inconceivable, so inhuman, that people reacted by showing what came to be known as the "Ermua spirit". The Ermua spirit was the way society, citizens, and several political organizations decided to put an end to that disgrace. Nationalism was overcome by an outpouring of freedom, and for a moment it prospered. If that spirit had continued and kept inspiring all of the Basque Country's political forces, things would have turned out very differently. But, unfortunately, that wasn't the case. On the exact same day as the demonstration against the murder of Miguel Ángel Blanco, the nationalists decided to put an end to the Ermua spirit.

The Victims of Terror

Terrorism has only one cause, regardless of where or in what situation it arises: fanaticism. Whether it's ethnic, nationalist or religious fundamentalism, it's always the desire to annihilate another. The match that lights the terrorist flame is always the same, regardless of circumstances.

I can never forget that I am privileged. I was lucky enough to survive an attempt on my life. That means I have a special responsibility to the victims of terror. That's inevitable, and it's much stronger than any personal decision. My stance against terrorism has political and democratic foundations, legal and moral motives. The moral basis is directly related to the obligation I feel towards the victims of terror.

People who have suffered terrorist attacks are the most important thing of all. They have to be at the center of any counter-terrorist policy. They are the ones who have suffered and they are also a testimony to human dignity in the face of barbarity.

I don't think victims in Spain have been treated well. They've had to face a triple humiliation. First, as victims of an attack. Second, they face the humiliation of insult, which the victims of terrorism are often subjected to in the Basque Country. And third, in addition to insult, they are then forgotten. We had to do something on that third point. It was vital that we make a radical change. We had to recognize the victims of terrorism and give them the honor and dignity they deserved for the moral strength and patriotism they had shown.

We fought for an international forum for victims of terrorism, for an organization to represent them. We sponsored this initiative at United

Nations headquarters in New York. And in 2003 at the United Nations - an organization dedicated to the defense of human rights - the victims of terror spoke out for the first time, giving their testimony.

For a long time, a lot of people didn't want to tackle the issue head-on. They preferred to look the other way. But that's no way to solve problems. Problems can only be solved if you face up to them directly. It's harder and it's riskier, but it's the only way. Spain won't be able to eradicate terrorism until we dare to stare it in the face, with no fear.

While it's true that individual shows of solidarity and commitment are becoming stronger and stronger, we also needed to change the character of our political leadership. If people have doubts about a leader's position, they'll tend to ask themselves why they have to assume risks that others aren't willing to take on. So we had to make it very clear and put the people who had suffered from terrorism right at the center of our plan.

The steps we've taken over these years, such as the Basta Ya! (That's Enough!) campaign, the Ermua Forum and the Foundation for Freedom are proof of the fact that society can and will band together to take a stance against terrorism. They prove the bravery and commitment of those who refuse to live under a reign of terror, threats and blackmail. Day-to-day survival is the hardest part of it, daring to walk on the streets knowing that they're there, watching you, and seeing that some people refuse to speak out in the face of that. If people don't react, if society doesn't take responsibility for its convictions, then it's a whole lot harder, and so is taking any government action.

I would have liked more commitment, an even greater show of strength. We always gave the Socialists our support, as was fitting, and gave them total freedom, too. We never made any distinctions between who came from one side and who came from another, who was Popular Party and who was Socialist. The only line we drew was between terrorists and democrats.

I have always attended the funerals of those killed by terrorists. I decided to do that because I felt it was an obligation as government leader. I have only not gone when families insisted that they preferred a strictly private affair. Aside from that, I went, regardless of the victim's position, occupation or political ideology. It's not just a symbolic act; it's an obligation: it's my duty, and it's only natural given our counter-terrorism policy and our manifest desire to give victims the dignity they deserve.

I have passed too many folded flags and placed too many medals on too many coffins in the past few years. I've also buried a lot of fellow party members, a lot of good people, good people who shouldn't have suffered this terrible violence. It's been hard, but it was my duty.

These are terrible, awful times, with intense emotions. But you have to hold back, you can't fall apart because in those circumstances you have an incredible responsibility. You cannot forget that you are what you represent at a time like that. People have just suffered an act of terrorism and they need to feel the decorum and the moral rectitude of your intentions. Their faith is critical; they must have no doubt about what you're telling them.

I've never wanted there to be any doubt about that. We've never made or maintained any contact with the terrorist world, except when I took direct responsibility, which I'll explain later. We knew that you couldn't distinguish between a terrorist organization and its purportedly non-violent setting. It's all the same. We had to act against them all, and although we also had to defend people's political opportunities, we've always had an all-encompassing policy against terrorist action and anyone who supports terrorism, in Spain or abroad.

I can recall one particularly terrible moment after Manuel Zamarreño was assassinated. He had been Popular Party Councilor in the Basque village of Rentería. He was murdered in June 1998. In 1997 fourteen people were assassinated. And by the time of Zamarreño's murder, they had killed so many: Gregorio Ordóñez and Miguel Ángel Blanco in July 1997; José Luis Caso was killed in December 1997; Jose Ignacio Iruretagoyena in January 1998; Alberto Jiménez Becerril and his wife Ascensión García Ortiz, both also in January 1998; and Tomás Caballero, United People of Navarra Councilor, in May 1998. Alfonso Parada, Civil Guard Second Lieutenant, was also murdered in 1998.

After Zamarreño's murder we held a meeting and then a luncheon in a Guipúzcoa hotel. The party had suffered a tremendous blow: six murders in a row. About two hundred people, all from the Popular Party, attended the meeting, and I felt them all looking at me. Their faces showed profound anguish, although they also showed heroism. These were people whose behavior embodies the full scope of human greatness. I knew what they were saying: we don't know how this is going to continue or how it's going to end, but those of us who are here know that we'll never all be together again. Earlier, they had approached me in a show of emotion and said, "Stay with us; promise us you'll always be close by, that you won't go far."

That calls for a personal response. They had to see that their leader not only wasn't going to be defeated but that he would remain steadfast and moral and put on a brave face. But we also needed a political response. And that response should have been to tell them not to worry because we'd put an end to this. But that was exactly what we couldn't say. The only thing we could do was tell them to hang in there, not to cave in. That was an incredibly difficult moment, one of the hardest things I've lived through.

That all came back to me last month in San Sebastian. It was six years after José Ignacio Iruretagoyena had been murdered. María San Gil, who had been right there when Gregorio Ordóñez was shot and who is an extraordinarily courageous woman, recalled the tragedy and suddenly their absences were palpable, enormous. The intensity of that experience is something I felt when I made a firm decision. I will never abandon my friends in the Basque Country. I'll always be there for them, through thick and thin.

The 2001 Elections: A Long Uphill Battle

The results of the May 2001 local elections were another difficult time, but that was more due to political disappointment than any terrorist demands. The Popular Party and the PSOE had reached a basic agreement, thanks to Jaime Mayor Oreja and Nicolás Redondo Terreros. We had to stand together to fight the Estrella Pact, signed in 1998 by the Basque National Party, HB (Herri Batisuna) and the United Left, which in essence came down on the side of ETA.

Spaniards had made great strides in their support for the Constitution and the Autonomous Communities. And because the Basque Country had become an autonomous state, they had more self-government than ever before. There are Basque chartered institutions, they have their own fiscal agreement that allows them a lot of autonomy, and there is a Basque police force. Today, Basque expressions of culture – language, arts of all types – are respected, supported, and widely distributed. Every idea, every opinion, every project finds expression.

The Basque nationalist response, however, was not constructive. Rather than make any contributions to this common cultural endeavor, the nationalists had dug their heels in and seemed committed to cutting themselves off even more. What's more, they'd tried to impose a unilateral vision of the Basque Country and had no qualms about reaching agreements with groups that had collaborated with terrorists. So it came as no surprise that those who had always opposed this now wanted to see the terrorists and their supporters defeated in the elections.

What's more, people who hoped that being an Autonomous Community would facilitate peace and freedom couldn't believe that a lot of the Basque Nationalist Party, people who seemed reasonably democratic and open to dialogue on many issues, could be so callous as to not show a shred of human feeling when it came to things like the results of terrorist violence.

And there's one more factor that explains our optimism in the

2001 election campaign. That was the very human belief that Basque society, part of Spain and part of Europe, couldn't just sit back and accept what was happening.

All of that understandably generated extraordinary confidence, and it was very difficult to respond to that enthusiasm by saying that the alternative in the Basque Country was going to be a long, hard road, that it would take a long time to build. And that was how the idea of actually going out to win came about. It was inevitable. Jaime Mayor Oreja, who'd left the Ministry of the Interior to become our candidate, said that we had to go out and try to win those elections, and I accepted his proposal. But the truth is that I never thought we'd win.

I thought it was already pretty amazing that after everything that had happened, we'd gotten as far as we had in the Basque Country, and that there were many people who thought we could defeat the nationalists at the polls. Keep in mind that nationalists have been in power since 1980. What's more, when there had been a chance to take back the government, we hadn't done it. We'd turned down the opportunity, like in the 1986 elections. That's not a criticism. There's no doubt it was a goodwill effort that was made in the hopes of ending terrorism. But the fact is, it ended up putting the Basque Nationalist Party in power.

So it was very unlikely that we would then win the May 2001 elections. Despite the tragedy of everything that had happened, despite the climate that had been created, it was still an incredible long shot to think that on our first try, we could actually go out and change things once and for all, undo what had been done for twenty-one years. In the long run, terrorism subverts all of a society's moral values. That's what it's done in the Basque Country. And the allegedly moderate nationalism hasn't helped the situation; in fact, it's made it worse.

So that's where we stood in the run-up to the elections. We pulled out all the stops in an attempt to win. But what really mattered was that the next day, when the results came in, we had to avoid a crushing disappointment. That's why I explained that we'd been closer than ever, and though it was tough to admit we hadn't turned things around, we had to face up to it and move on, just keep on in the effort.

That's why, immediately after the polls closed, I told everyone – all the people and the groups working for us – that regardless of the outcome there was no way we were going to be defeated after what had happened here. I said we had to carry on, because this was tough and it was going to be a long, hard road. They had to know they could count on the government to act, know that we weren't going to change, that we'd keep up our efforts and, if necessary, redouble them. Someone asked me if there was a Plan B, in case we lost the elections. But there was only a Plan A, which was to propose an alternative and to win, whether in the short-term or the long-term, but win.

I know it's hard to keep that up, and that's exactly why I have made certain that that's the Popular Party's everyday position. I knew there could be an upset, and after all it's much easier to relay messages like, "We have to be flexible, we have to be open to dialogue." But when it comes down to it, that's worthless. I was crystal clear on that point. If the Socialists didn't agree, then we could follow that course of action alone. I'd rather do it together, especially given the circumstances, but we were willing to go it alone if necessary. It would be much harder, but that was what we had to do.

The May 2001 elections were the first time the nationalists felt the anguish of a possible defeat. They'd been hearing that the Basque Country was theirs for a long time; that there was no alternative and if there was an alternative it wasn't democratic, because democracy in the Basque Country is associated with the nationalists. Anything that isn't nationalist is seen as anti-Basque. That's why the nationalists treated those elections like a foreign invasion and appealed to people's most basic emotions.

In Search of an Alternative

The only alternative is to keep slogging away. We have to make everyone who saw the possibility of an alternative as some far-off prospect begin to see it as a reality. And that means we have to keep up a continuous political presence and effort.

It was obvious that the Socialists had to shift closer to the Popular Party's position, and that's what they did with the antiterrorist pact: the Accord For Freedom and Against Terrorism, signed in December 2000. But the Socialists were very cautious in their approach and tried to differentiate themselves. After all, the Socialists were predicting a possible return to power, so it was in their interest to leave the door open to the possibility of some sort of arrangement with the nationalists. That's exactly what led, later, to discussions about the Spanish state model and constitutional reform.

Another thing that the Socialist stance led to was Nicolás Redondo Terreros' resignation as Secretary General of the PSOE in the Basque Country, in December 2001, just six months after the elections. There were various excuses given, such as his having come to see me alone. But the truth is that one part of the PSOE disagreed with Nicolás Redondo and thought they needed to differentiate themselves from the Popular Party; they thought that their proximity to us could hurt them politically, and they wanted to leave themselves open to talks with the nationalists, in case it was in their interests further down the line.

After the 1996 elections we weren't reliant on any pacts with the Basque Nationalist Party to form our government. We decided to include them for two reasons. First, because it was the chance to set right some historical misunderstandings that we could finally, definitively leave behind, given that we were no longer in the same situation. And also, we had to try to work with the Basque Nationalists to improve the situation. That was our approach, and the whole pact and negotiation process were conducted entirely out in the open, with complete transparency.

At the time, the Basque Nationalist Party defended the Ajuria Enea Pact and claimed to agree with it. Then they changed their minds and decided, first, to end the goodwill spirit that had arisen after Miguel Ángel Blanco's assassination, which meant they had to radically distance themselves from any non-nationalist option; then they had to ally themselves with every nationalist current, including Herri Batasuna and their friends in the United Left. That's what they did in the Estrella Pact, signed in September 1998.

We made an attempt to reconcile with them in 1996. But there's only so far you can go. A lot of people told me, later, that I should have made more of an effort, been more flexible, entered into dialogue. Ironically, I think the people who said that the most were the same ones who later reproached me for having talked to the Basque Nationalist Party in 1996 at all. But when people and parties don't want to budge, there's not much you can do. Santiago Carrillo took part in the celebrations for the 25th anniversary of the Constitution, held on the date of the signing of the Declaration of Gredos in October 2003. But Gaspar Llamazares, for example, was not present, which meant that the United Left wasn't represented. Nor was the Basque Nationalist Party. At some point, a decision had been made that it was impossible to defeat terrorism. We had to disprove that.

The Basque Nationalist Party didn't want to defeat ETA. Every time ETA has been backed into a corner, the Basque Nationalists have thrown them a lifeline. That's what they did with the campaign they organized in opposition to the Leizarán highway, and then again when key ETA leaders were detained in Bidart, in 1992.

The Basque Nationalist Party props up the myth that it's impossible to defeat terrorism, and they do it because they're convinced that the defeat of ETA would mean the defeat of nationalism. But their strategy came to a head when, after Miguel Ángel Blanco was murdered in 1997, the nationalist position was nearly refuted by what was going on. That's when, suddenly, they come out with a new line: terrorism can be defeated, and we'll do it ourselves. How? Simple: by telling ETA they were right, which just reinforced nationalist unity, as seen by the September 1998 Estrella Pact.

After a trial that began in 1996, all twenty-three members of Herri Batasuna's national committee were imprisoned for seven years; this was before we came to power. But then in a regrettable move, a constitutional court reversed the decision and released them in July 1999. There was absolutely no doubt that there were Herri Batasuna members directly implicated in ETA terrorism.

That was when Herri Batasuna was declared illegal by the Supreme Court, and when we decided to advance the measures eventually expressed in the Law of Political Parties, approved by Parliament in June 2002. That was a personal matter. I asked a lot of people for their opinions and most of them, for opportunistic reasons, were opposed. To me, however, it was a crucial move. And I wanted to make it comprehensive by enacting penal reforms to ensure that full sentences were served, terrorist crimes and street violence were classified, and the parents of young people who were involved in these activities were held accountable. From that moment on we haven't had to suffer the shame of having to see terrorists seated on the bench in Parliament. We told the Socialists, and although neither the United Left nor the Catalan Convergència I Unió party came on board, the PSOE did, and that was enough to get the reforms through.

The Batasuna honchos are now what they should be: illegal. Why was that the right moment for this action? Because I was convinced that the social change we were trying to promote had already taken place. People had changed their way of thinking about terrorism. In Spain, there used to be a general consensus that Batasuna should be allowed to exist legally if we wanted to fight terrorism.

I never believed that, but in order to do anything about it people had to see that a general consensus could change. Even if it hadn't made a complete turnaround, it had begun in a substantial portion of the population and that meant it was possible. By then I was convinced that by setting the initiative in motion, it would reach a consensus. I was also sure that the threats about the Basque Country being burned to the ground if Batasuna were declared illegal were baseless. And they were. So the Supreme Court's decision ended up being very positive.

The so-called "kale borroka" (Basque for "street violence") has almost disappeared and terrorism has suffered a terrible blow. Jaime

Mayor Oreja, Mariano Rajoy and Ángel Acebes have done an incredible job. The Civil Guard, the national police and the information services have worked extraordinarily hard over the past years. I have borne witness to their amazing work in a field in which people often don't get the recognition they deserve. And I am deeply proud of them.

As I said before, if the PSOE hadn't joined us on that initiative we'd have pushed it through ourselves. I have my own convictions and I know not everyone shares them. What matters is that the action taken benefits the country as a whole. The Socialists have had it very hard in the Basque Country; they've suffered a lot and their losses there have been as painful as ours. As far as I'm concerned, you don't distinguish between victims.

However, the Socialists had a coalition government with the Basque Nationalist Party in the Basque Country. They have worked together and the Socialists have enjoyed a certain degree of institutional protection. Overturning that would be very hard and very costly. That's why I made my position clear from day one. It was non-negotiable, but I hoped the Socialists would come on board.

Obviously, we knew our policy would have several consequences. First, it would have tremendously positive effects on people's peace of mind. The days of impunity were over. People would know that from then on, criminals were acting outside the law rather than being protected by it. That was a basic, moral issue. From a political perspective, that change signified a rejection of the idea that the Basque Country belonged to the nationalists and that terrorists would be protected under democratic law there. Neither the Constitution nor the Statute could be used to help criminals run free. The time had come to say enough is enough. If the Socialists were opposed, democratically that was a legitimate option, but they'd have some explaining to do in terms of public opinion.

The Estrella Pact was part of the same movement that began with the ETA "ceasefire" in 1998. From a counter-terrorist perspective, as far as we were concerned there was no ceasefire. All counter-terrorist operations carried on as planned that summer. And politically speaking, there was a lot to consider. Personally, I had so little faith in their declaration that my first reaction was one of contempt.

Then people convinced me not to be so categorical in my condemnation. Because even if I had no faith in their gesture, we shouldn't let the possible hopes that some people felt be dashed. So at the time I accepted it, and agreed to consider the possibility on two conditions. First, I would be personally responsible. And second, everything had to be done with complete transparency and we had to tell people exactly what we were doing, without holding anything back. No secrets.

It turned out that those of us who'd thought that the whole thing was just a political move were right. In fact, the terrorists were worried about the 1998 elections in the Basque Country and wanted a chance to restructure internally. The strategy failed, because the election results weren't what they had hoped for and ETA went out and murdered again. But we had to prove that there was never really any intention of putting an end to the violence. We never told anything but the truth. We had no contracts, no conversations with them aside from those we've disclosed, and they were all held under the terms we've made public. And we all know how things turned out.

A Word on Dialogue

We'd been fighting for years to make changes internationally on things like police cooperation, legislation and classifying terrorist groups. And just a few months after September 11th, we achieved more than we had over the course of all those years. The Spanish government was in a very strong position since we were recognized as moral leaders in the fight against terror. Suddenly we received full cooperation and understanding on issues of international protection, investigating terrorist financing, and taking the necessary steps to penetrate the terrorists' environment. Some countries cooperated out of conviction and others because they realized that they had no choice but to face up to the world we now live in. But they all did it.

But September 11th had no bearing on the Basque Nationalist Party's political decision. Quite the opposite, in fact, because their previous course of action actually sped up at that point, and led to what they called the Ibarretxe Plan. Once the Estrella Pact failed, and once they saw the international reaction – and particularly the European reaction – to September 11th, the Basque Nationalist Party just decided to put this plan into action, the same way they'd decided to put an end to the Ermua spirit.

In actual fact, it was the same old story. To put an end to terrorism you supposedly have to sit down and talk, negotiate, come to a political agreement. But the guns are always on the coffee table, or on the arm of the sofa, while you're talking. And if necessary, they'll shoot people in the back. As far as the nationalists are concerned, putting an end to the violence, putting away the guns, is never part of the commitment. The commitment is what ensures that the guns get to make decisions and that's what you get when you start talks under those kinds of conditions.

Sometimes, when people talk about dialogue, they don't seem to realize that they're putting the Spanish government and the terrorists on the same level; they're saying we should go ahead with dialogue under the threat of violence. I've never done that. We are not on the same level, and there is no possible halfway mark, no conceivable middle ground between us.

If the dialogues are about the transfer of powers, that's one thing. We're prepared to talk as much as necessary about that. But let's not be mistaken. The talks I've had proposed to me had nothing to do with the running of the Autonomous Communities. The talks proposed to me were about negotiating a date for the end of Spain. You can't ask any head of government to sit down at the table and actually draw up a timeline for the secession of part of Spain.

The only difference between ETA and the Basque Nationalist Party on this is the deadline. ETA wants the Basque Country to secede the day after tomorrow and the Basque Nationalist Party wants to give it five or six months. But they're both after the same thing; they both want it all and just differ on the terms. So there's nothing to talk about.

If we're going to have dialogue, it has to be loyal to our institutions, to the Constitution, to the legitimacy that has allowed nationalists to rule in the Basque Country for the past twenty-three years, to the consensus we're reaching on the constitutional text and the Statute of Autonomy. That, we can sit down at the table about. Not the other. I have nothing to say about the destruction of Spain.

The government and its leader have had to pay a price for insisting on that. Our clarity and our decision to stand firm have led to the idea that we're inflexible, intransigent. But it's important to keep in mind that any negotiations on this matter lead to acknowledging self-determination, and that leads to secession.

Most of the country agrees with our position. What we need is for them to realize that it's also their concern, a concern that no one can resolve for them. People have actually already started to realize that. They know it's Spain's number one problem and they're not willing to hand the country over to anyone who won't ensure that secession never occurs.

The only risk here is the possibility of some people thinking it's a personal stance, that it's just the way José María Aznar feels. In fact, it's a national concern. My resigning from government, and from the Popular Party, is aimed at showing that this is not the case. The fight against terror and the refusal to sit down to talks with terrorists and all those who use violence to advance their positions is not a personal matter. It's a national, institutional matter. The Popular Party knows that it has to respond to the majority opinion. Especially when the going gets tough. This must be made perfectly clear.

It's possible that within the Basque Country, and even beyond its borders, people could become disenchanted, even fed up. That would be like giving up, surrendering to the violence the people there are subjected to and that makes them move away. Without people, the whole ship sinks. That's why reestablishing a modicum of normality in people's everyday existence there is so vital. That's why they have to know that the government and the rest of the country support them. So we also have to do something to assure the functioning of normal democratic order.

We've done everything in our power to help and to support all those who haven't yielded to nationalism. We have absolutely respected the Basque educational freedom as delineated in the Statutes, and we have reformed educational curricula to the degree possible. We've published and promoted new history books and historical studies; we've backed social initiatives such as the associations created in the Basque Country and the rest of Spain. We've helped people; sometimes we've even given them professional opportunities when the threats and harassment reached unbearable limits.

But the main thing is that we've tried to recover moral values, instill in people – especially the victims of terror – the ideas and moral support necessary to keep them from feeling cut off. In some parts of the Basque Country, the Spanish flag hadn't waved in years. Now it does.

The problems can be solved if a majority of the country feels it's worth doing. The roots of Spain grow deep, a lot deeper than people sometimes think. There may be some uncertainty, but what matters is that we not let the uncertainty degenerate into apathy. That's why we have to measure our response very carefully. In politics, the right decision at the wrong time is a failure.

The way I see it, the current response is insufficient, because people won't believe in the alternative in the Basque Country until they see it as feasible. It should be as broad a coalition as possible, but if there is no choice but to go it alone, working year after year, month after month, day after day, for the support of the majority, then that's what we'll do. We must work within the constraints of the law, without pushing any deadlines, knowing that this is a long-term project and that we'll have to draft political responses to issues as the opportunities arise.

I mean what I say literally. The Ibarretxe Plan has no chance whatsoever. Literally, zero. People can draw whatever conclusions they want from that.

An International Fight

The whole world respects, endorses and supports the Spanish government's fight against terrorism. The whole world agrees that the idea of the Basque Country seceding is inconceivable, especially considering that we're talking about Spain, a member of the European Union. It's a matter that doesn't even enter into international discussions.

France's cooperation has improved substantially over the years. There's always room for improvement, but if you consider French aid now with their line back in the Seventies, it's reasonably positive.

One thing that's fundamental is for the United Nations to establish a global list of terrorist organizations, even if it's not easy. It doesn't have to include every terrorist organization there is, but it needs to take account of all those organizations that we now agree, by consensus, are terrorist organizations. Then as new consensuses are reached, the list can continue to grow. That way the UN will have the chance to demonstrate a hard-line stance in defense of the human rights that are threatened by terrorism.

This list should be comparable to the United States' list, given their leadership role in the fight against international terror. That's fundamental. We must be unwavering in our support of the United States, and vice versa.

Everyone has to realize that terrorism is the always the same, regardless of where it crops up; all terrorists are the same and should all be treated the same. Terrorism is a response to particular historical situations in every country, yes, but just as there are no specific causes for terrorism, there is also no justification for violence or the violation of basic human rights. As I've already said, all terrorism ultimately stems from fanaticism, fundamentalism, sectarianism and the desire to annihilate the adversary.

Terrorists can allege whatever they want as justification for their actions, but the basic root cause is always the same and has no possible justification. Nowadays, people talk a lot about poverty as a means of explaining terrorist action. Poverty is unacceptable and we have to use all of our resources to put an end to it. But that doesn't explain the emergence of terrorism.

ETA is not the face of the dispossessed in the Basque Country. Nor is the IRA in Ireland. The Red Brigades in Italy were not born of misery, and nor were Baader Meinhof, Bin Laden or the Al Qaeda network. In fact, in places that are overcome by real destitution, such as much of Africa, you have no terrorist threat. There are other grave, extremely urgent problems, but not that one.

You do, on the other hand, find terrorism in places with fundamentalist politics, such as Marxism, or ethnic, religious or nationalist fundamentalism. Terrorism is a weapon brandished in an attempt to annihilate an adversary or a dissident. And September 11th proved that it can strike anywhere in the world.

That's why we can't allow terrorism in some places but not in others. If we do, we incapacitate the international fight against terror, first, and then we weaken national efforts against it, too. Just as there is no justification for terrorism, there is also no place we are safe from it.

A United Nations emissary, a good man, once told me he wanted to ask for my help on something. I said I would be happy to lend a hand in any way I could. And then he asked me to support the defense of human rights in ... the United States. So then I had to ask him if he really thought that the West, and particularly the United States, was where human rights were in danger.

We might need more explanations about what the fight against terror really entails, and some measures might be open to discussion, just as some might be abused. But in all honesty, I don't think that we are facing any threat to our freedom and security. Except from terrorism, of course. A lot of people's lives are at risk there, and our freedom, our very civilization is in danger. In the United States, as in Spain and the rest of the democratic world, it's not the liberal democracies that are posing the threat to freedom and human rights.

That's why we need a forum for the victims of terror at the United Nations. That forum acts as a way of literally making the human rights violations visible. Here we have the father, the wife, the brother of a victim of terrorist action. Here we have someone who's been mutilated, someone who lost their children, or who saw their professional life ended forever by fanaticism. That's what matters. And provided we keep the real threat in mind, if we're clear on that, then we can discuss whatever is necessary.

CHAPTER EIGHT

Constitutional Spain

Just before Christmas, in December 2003, I paid a visit to the Spanish troops in Diwaniyah, Iraq. The day before, I'd had a videoconference with members of our armed forces stationed in Bosnia, Kosovo, Afghanistan, Abu Dhabi and Djibouti. I wanted to let them know I was with them all the way, but there's no substitute for direct contact.

I came back from Iraq proud and satisfied. Our soldiers were there for security measures, but they were also part of the reconstruction effort and to help humanitarian aid. The factories in the region are already back up and running again. They had electricity for seventeen to eighteen hours a day. The people had the supplies they needed. And in terms of the political process, there were great hopes for the future thanks to the capture of Saddam Hussein. I don't think there's any way that the previous rulers will return to power.

Our soldiers performed magnificently. Their spirits were high, and their dedication and commitment superb. They followed all the rules, they knew exactly what needed to be done and they had a very good relationship with the locals. They worked in partnership with Latin American troops, who they told me were well-prepared and working under skilled commanders. The Iraqis are happy with our soldiers. I met with a few important people from the region, and their expressions of gratitude were unanimous; they all valued the Spanish effort. All Spaniards should feel proud of our troops.

Twenty-First Century Nationalism

People say we're suffering from a nationalist offensive in Spain right now. In my opinion, this phenomenon derives from three factors, two of which are general and one specific, although it has historical origins.

The first general factor is the autonomic state model set out in the 1978 Constitution. The State of Autonomies has been growing and developing since the signing of the Constitution and, as set out in the constitutional text, has facilitated tremendous decentralization and transfer of powers. The Autonomous Community governments have taken on increasing powers and responsibilities. Now, in 2004, we've reached the end of that process. We've achieved the maximum level of self-government possible within the constitutional framework. And, given that, the political forces at play have begun to adopt positions.

The second general factor is the European framework. The European Union is the culmination of several processes: the single currency was created and the Treaty of Nice achieved a certain degree of much-needed harmony for the institutional construction of a twenty-five-member Europe. There is still a lot that needs to be outlined and that will be the subject of future negotiations, but the plan is set for several years. And the plan is for a Europe made up of strong, stable nation states. A lot of people, in particular the nationalists, were hoping for a Europe in which nation states were watered down. Well, the Europe we've got is not a post-national Europe; it's a Union of solid nation states. And that means we need to adopt positions for the future.

The third factor is the specific one, and it has to do with the evolution of the PSOE, which I'll go into later.

These are the three factors we need to take into consideration to understand this "nationalist offensive" we're undergoing. One historic process is drawing to a close and another is just beginning. Now Spaniards have before them a decision, they have to opt for one of two possibilities. One: we're tired of everything we've done over the past twenty-five years, and we think the effects haven't been beneficial to the country so we opt for a different model. Or two: we think the stability and continuity begun in 1978 are worth the effort.

My position is clear. I'm convinced that we ought to continue the process begun with the Constitution in 1978. In the last two hundred years, Spaniards have had a lack of stability that has led to all sorts of problems, inequalities within the country, and exceedingly painful conflicts. Even the historic continuity of our country was in doubt.

So now the question is: do we want to go back to our old ways, keep tripping over the same cracks in the sidewalk, and take a path that we know will leave us in the same old place? Or do we, on the other hand, want to stay on the road of stability, freedom, prosperity, opportunities and progress for the country? Those are the questions we now face.

The Socialists' Failings

As things stand, the Socialists have me very worried. The feeling of there being a nationalist offensive doesn't derive so much from their actions as from their failings. It's a big problem when a national party, as the PSOE is or should be, bows to nationalist pressure. Instead of acting as a backbone for the state and the nation, as is their duty as a national party, they've caved in to the pressure of nationalism and are becoming spokespeople for nationalist movements.

There are several reasons for this. After the fall of the Berlin Wall and then later with the phenomenon of globalization and the consequences of September 11th, the left lost most of its ideological reference points. It's clear that the left needs to go through a major overhaul, reexamining its proposals and visions, and it's obvious that it hasn't yet begun to do so, at least in Spain.

When they show no analytical ability, when a party is totally out of touch with reality, there is surely also a concurrent lack of internal convictions, which are needed to confront new problems. The PSOE's lack of convictions has become evident in their stance, especially during this last term. I think it's essential that there are alternatives; that's vital to a democracy. And those that are backed by the electorate are put into action. But opposition parties also have responsibilities, especially if they want to govern.

There are some major issues related to the very structure of the state, the roots of the nation, which should never be a bone of contention between political parties. Besides, the Socialists have made substantial contributions to our national history over the last twenty-five years. They were key players in the transition and the drafting of the Constitution, and they were in power for nearly fourteen years. So they're no strangers to what's been going on in Spain.

Unfortunately, however, rather than offer alternatives on common ground, they have chosen an extremist tack, as they did in the Iraq War by siding with the United Left. They've also chosen to make alliances with groups on the fringes of the democratic system, thereby lending those groups the credibility they lack.

A national party, regardless of its ideology, can't renounce its national characteristic. When, during the 1996-2000 term, the Socialists voted against reforms in the teaching of the Humanities, that's what they did, and it was a terrible mistake. When they opposed the Hydrological Plan that's what they did; when they opposed the model for pensions that's what they did. A national party, and a national party on the left no less, cannot be opposed to distributing such a precious resource as water. Nor can they be opposed to a country's history - Spain's history - being taught all over the country. Likewise, they can't back a system that sets up different pensions, unequal pensions, according to region, an incredibly expensive system that hinders the domestic mobility of our population.

The internal failings of the PSOE also reflect eight years of distancing themselves from power. During this period, as I've said, I have had five different opposition speakers. At first they couldn't believe they'd lost. I think they still haven't really accepted it. And yet the country has enjoyed stability and growth throughout these years.

We've seen increasing prosperity and we have an increasingly vital presence on the world stage. The transition was successful and so was the process it set in motion. It's been a long phase, incomparable to any other in our history. Our progress is proven by the numbers - concrete data - as we've seen. It's something we can be proud of.

That's why it's especially sad and risky that just at this moment, out of either a lack of convictions or political opportunism, the opposition would attempt to question the basic building blocks that allowed this progress to occur. There are a lot of contradictions coming out of the PSOE right now; they're not being constructive and when they do something explicit, it becomes obvious that they're proposing just what we shouldn't do. Because they are proposing nothing less than regime change. And that means the number one problem they face right now is themselves.

The Culmination of the State of Autonomies

In the eight years of Popular Party government, we've seen the culmination of the State of Autonomies reform process. I've already said that it's something I helped start when I was young, even before I embarked on my political career. Then, in 1992, I signed the Autonomous Pact with the Socialists because it was logical that, as national parties, we both agree on the transfer of powers to the Autonomous Communities as set out in Article 147. That's how the synchronization process for the statutes of all of the Autonomous Communities began. And that's why we've had a transfer of powers, as laid out by the Constitution, that began with the PSOE and since 1996 has continued under the Popular Party.

In terms of financing, the Popular Party has reached two Autonomous Community finance agreements, one in each term. The second set up a system backed by every Community. In the past eight years, the Catalan government – the Generalitat – has seen its budget increase by 70%. Today the Generalitat handles a three-billion-peseta budget. If you look at that per capita, it's the same as the national budget. For every hundred Euros the state spends, more than fifty are spent on local administration, including the armed forces, the justice system and pensions.

We've also reformed the Statutes of Autonomy during this time. We always helped carry out all of the reforms on two conditions. First, that they follow the statutory reform procedures initially agreed upon, that is, under the broadest possible coalition of political parties. And second, that the reforms be specific enough to benefit the overall population. That's what we've done over these years. What we haven't done, what we didn't want to do and refuse to do, is modify the actual structure of the system, the rules of the game that allow for its smooth operation.

The transfer of powers went as far as it could go under our government. We're no longer at the stage of forming regional governments. Now, Autonomous Community governments need to administer their own authority to the benefit of their citizens, and the national government has to shoulder its responsibility to the country as a whole. Someone has to guarantee that the minimum criteria are met and establish the patterns to be followed in order to ensure the equal treatment of all Spanish citizens. That's the national government's responsibility; the national government must never renounce its essential powers of legislation and organization.

Well, that's exactly what the Socialists have done with the pact they've signed with the Catalan government, made up of the Catalan Socialist Party and the Catalan Left. To begin with, it's a political anomaly, since it gives a small, local party the power to change the rules of the constitutional game that affect the entire country. But in addition to that, this is part of a project that extends far beyond the powers of an Autonomous Community. What's at play here are the powers of self-determination, that is, secession, and that's an attack on everything that Spaniards have in common.

There is nothing positive behind this, nothing that could possibly benefit the country as a whole. The only thing they're doing with pacts like this one is rehearsing the disappearance of the state, the disappearance of fiscal administration, the dismantling of the judicial system, the fragmentation of the entire administration. They are destroying the fundamental notion of cooperation amongst Spaniards. The sort of project the Socialists are attempting to undertake - and then daring to claim that it doesn't pose a huge risk for the country - is absolutely astonishing.

There is only one stance the government can possibly take in the face of this, and that is to make it perfectly clear that the basic framework of the state cannot be touched. We can discuss whatever fine points you like. But there are certain basic, fundamental questions that are not open to discussion. One is the country's territorial unity. The domestic market is another, and that forms part of the single European market. And you can't undermine Social Security, a basic instrument of unity and equality. There has to be a common judicial system. Foreign security is part of the state's realm, both in terms of the armed forces and political representation. Guaranteeing that the law is obeyed everywhere is also a state responsibility. And finally there are certain elements of cultural cohesion that should be guaranteed by the state, such as the use of Spanish. These national powers are subjected to the authority of Parliament, which represents the people and has the power to legislate at the national level.

The Autonomous Communities are involved in a huge number of undertakings. Health and education have been transferred to them, as have some security forces, such as in the Basque Country and Catalonia. That proves what a decentralized system we've built.

People talk a lot about interregional cooperation, although we should really clear up what we mean by interregional and what we mean by cooperation. Regions don't pay taxes, and nor do regional or national administrations. People pay taxes and they are the ones who show their cooperation by doing so.

The same people who today are talking about cooperation are also proposing that the richest regions, like Catalonia and the Basque Country, contribute less than regions with lower income levels. To begin with, that's an unfair system, because it destroys the very concept of cooperation by which people pay taxes for the common good. We've tried to avoid a two-speed growth in Spain, that is, we've tried not to allow inequality between regions, which is something that's proved very damaging in other countries. We must not allow it to happen here. Though there may be apparent inequities in income levels and fiscal expenditure, you can't deduce from that that those who contribute the most receive the least and vice versa. We all benefit, because by rebalancing income we create infrastructure that we all take advantage of and we create new opportunities in the domestic market.

They're proposing an impossible system because it does away with the national framework, which is common to all of us. So under their plan everyone would just fight for their own interests without ever being able to reach any agreements.

I know the price the Popular Party has to pay for our stand on this. They call us inflexible, antiquated. The same old clichés. But those who repeat them would do themselves a favor if they ever asked what's more progressive, the creation of wealth or the hampering of it; the assurance of cooperation and equality for all Spaniards regardless of what Community they live in or measures that favor difference and inequality; showing curiosity and an interest in being open to anything or closing yourself off from it all. But since they'll never ask themselves these questions, I really don't care if they criticize me for defending Spain and the idea of Spain.

My idea of Spain is that of a pluralist nation, one of many constituencies. So it's the state's obligation, the Prime Minister's obligation, to guarantee the diversity of languages, the plurality of cultures, political and administrative decentralization, and self-rule in the Autonomous Communities.

The years when the State of Autonomies was being built are rich, fruitful and very important. But the state can't keep transferring powers indefinitely. Today, for example, only two out of every ten civil servants work for the state. The rest work for the Communities.

If those remaining two are transferred as well, there will be no state left, no idea of a political body that is Spain.

Really, we're seeing two seemingly opposing phenomena. Our national consciousness has grown and intensified over these years, reinforced by our progress and by Spain's position in the world. And, on the other hand, we've set a decentralized system, the State of Autonomies, in motion. We have to learn to keep the balance between the two.

The Consensus on Europe

Generally speaking, Spain's decision to join the European Community and then the Union was supported by a very broad consensus. A huge majority associated –rightly so – the modernization of Spain with joining Europe, that is, the single market and European institutions. This is still the case.

Without forgetting this consensus, it's important to recognize that there were differences between some of the positions.

First, the nationalists tended to see it like this: the more we support Europe, the less there is for Spain. As nation states joined Europe, they would become weaker, and then there would be a historic opportunity not so much for the Autonomous Communities as for the nationalists. This would be their chance to turn what they saw as a nation without a recognized state into a fully-fledged country.

The left, too, had a slightly different position. They saw the national consciousness as weak, and therefore saw joining Europe as a means of compensating this lack of national consciousness. So the more involved in Europe we were, the better equipped we'd be to tackle our own domestic problems as they arose. Europe would help us solve the problems we couldn't face up to on our own.

The third position was ours. For me, the better off Spain is, the better for Europe. In other words, the stronger our national consciousness, our country, our sphere of influence, the more we can contribute to the European project and the stronger the Union itself will be. That shouldn't be seen as a purely European stance, either. It should be seen as a global perspective on foreign policy. If Spain's strategic position in the world is clearly defined, the country will never be lacking in possibilities for the future.

Those are the three outlooks that made up the general consensus on Spain's position in Europe. And over the years, they've coexisted in relative harmony. But a new situation began to arise in 2000. The new situation is what I've already outlined: first, the process of creation of the State of Autonomies was completed; and second, the Europe we've created is not post-national, it's based on the existence of strong, stable nation states.

So where do we go from here? Some people think we should substantially alter the country's political regime. They must also realize that they're proposing a substantial change in the European political map because if their plan were to move forward we'd have to change borders, countries and some of the institutional structures that the Union is built on, as a union of nation states. Backing a Europe not based on nation states has always been equivalent to setting ourselves up for failure. The idea of setting European interests in opposition to national interests is unthinkable.

What we had to do, and what we did, was reconcile national and European interests. That's why the British, French, Italians, Germans, and citizens of every other country want to keep being citizens of their countries and be European at the same time. This, along with the Atlantic Alliance guarantee, has been fundamental to the whole process; it's what's allowed a modern Europe with increasing world decision-making abilities, which requires great economic power.

In the end, it all comes down to a question of convictions. I believe in Spain, and I'm convinced that as part of Europe our country will become even stronger, and I'm sure that thanks to the Atlantic link, we'll have ever increasing opportunities.

But you can't look abroad, especially in the construction of the European Union, to try to hedge your bets, to cover up any lack of faith in your own country. Problems are only resolved when they're confronted, and the time has come to confront nationalism. Given where we are in our historical process, this is the time for those tensions to come to the fore. And Spain is capable, without a shadow of a doubt, of overcoming nationalism.

In Defense of the Constitution

Spain's constitutional model is alive and well. It's been extraordinarily successful in the past twenty-five years. No country would seriously consider the possibility of changing a Constitution that has guaranteed democracy, freedom, stability and economic progress for twenty-five years.

If specific amendments were proposed, we could discuss it, or at least try to understand what's behind the changes proposed. In 1992, Article 13.2 of the Constitution was adapted in consideration of the Treaties of the Union so that European citizens could stand in municipal elections. That was a very tangible reform, and all political parties supported it. But now all we know is that people are saying we have to change the Constitution because change would be modern, while refusing to change is inflexible. Well, we're not trying to argue about adjectives. What we need to do is explain why the Constitution should be changed, what benefit would it serve, what unforeseen situation that the constitutional text doesn't include would be covered by this reform.

That's when the reformers keep quiet. There is no clear reason, no argument, no need to reform the Constitution.

Right now, Spain has an extraordinary opportunity. You don't have to go too far back to see what we're talking about. Just look at the experiences of lots of Spaniards who know what things were like in 1978 and how they are now, in 2004. It's clear that the change has been so enormous that when people say we have to change the state's model, the most logical question is: why? Why go back through the whole process and risk all that we've accomplished and jeopardize the amazing opportunity we now have before us? Is it really worth it? Should we really destroy what's now on the horizon, put everything we've done over the past twenty-five years at risk and reopen discussions? We've stumbled over the same issues again and again, and thousands and thousands of Spaniards were condemned to live in far worse conditions than they would have if we'd just maintained historic continuity.

As far as I'm concerned, there's no reason to risk throwing all that away, none at all. I see no advantages whatsoever. To go back and reinitiate the process would be to start again, go back to how things were in 1978, to take a step back a quarter of a century. That's what proposing constitutional reform entails.

You can't just reform in one place because one group is having trouble forming a government with specific members, as occurred in Catalonia, and then think that the process ends there. If one Autonomous Community undertakes reforms, the whole process opens up and every Community can restart its own constituent process. The way I see it, that's exactly the opposite of what Spain needs. We need stability and historical continuity. Those are the foundations of serious countries.

As for the radical nationalist desire for Spain as we know it to disappear off the map, well that's just absurd. An independent's position is respectable on a theoretical level. We live in a free country and people can propose whatever they want. But a diametrically opposed conviction is also legitimate, and that's what mine is, and I'm convinced that most Spaniards agree.

Catalonian Nationalism

The Catalonian nationalist contribution to Spain's progress in the past twenty-five years of democracy has been essentially positive. They formed part of the constitutional consensus, helped draft the document, respected the law and showed a significant degree of commitment.

I do, however, have my differences with the course of action that the Catalonian nationalist government has taken. Why? The first reason is obvious: I'm not a nationalist, so even though I think that anything related to culture, customs and teaching their language is important and respectable, I also think that nothing about that requires a defensive stance. In fact, I think being defensive is harmful, not only to others but to themselves, because nationalism ends up closing itself off and acting as if there were nothing outside of its own identity.

But there's another reason. Catalonian nationalism had the chance to form part of the national government. They had an offer on the table in 1996 and another one in 2001, and we didn't actually need their parliamentary support to form a government. I'd known Jordi Pujol since I was President of Castilla y León, and back then he was saying that he could never make a pact with the Popular Party if they didn't have one more seat than the Socialists. Well, in 1996 we had not one but fifteen more.

After hearing the election results I spoke to Pujol, and that was when we first offered the Catalonian nationalists the chance to form part of the government. We put forward all sorts of reasons. We thought that the Constitution had given us the chance to heal old wounds, that we now had a common project, and that at the heart of Catalonian nationalism, as Cambó – one of its founders – had said, lay the aspiration for Catalonia to contribute decisively to the process of modernization and progress in Spain.

I told Pujol to think of Spain like a big forest, full of different types of trees. I said it was absurd to separate and divide the forest tree by tree, and that what we had to do was help the forest be as lush and rich and diverse as possible. And that we were there to help and to safeguard that project.

Even though they turned down the offer, we reached some agreements that ensured stability. It wasn't easy, but things went relatively smoothly and overall we've had a positive, fruitful partnership in Catalonia as in the rest of Spain. However, our initial blueprint for a steadfast partnership amongst all parties didn't really come to pass. In fact, I think we can identify a degree of vindictiveness in the emergence of the most radical forces.

I would have liked the Popular Party to play a more active role in Catalonia. But our trajectory hasn't been as consistent as we'd have liked and we've had some instability. Now the Popular Party is beginning to take on its own shape, with specific positions and projects in Catalonia. In my opinion, we'll become increasingly significant and welcomed there.

Basque Nationalism

In 1996 we didn't need the Basque Nationalist Party's help to form a majority. But, as I said, we wanted to reach an agreement with the nationalists so we could finally let bygones be bygones. It wasn't necessary, I repeat, either for investiture or for government stability, but we still reached an agreement and laid out the terms of cooperation that best served all of our interests. That's why we renewed the economic agreement, which was hugely important to the Basque Country, and it was renewed again this term.

I remember my conversations with Arzalluz and Ardanza well. They were long, difficult talks, but we managed to set out very precise limitations. I told them very clearly what we were willing to do. We were willing to help out on specific measures for progress, improvement and the exploitation of resources. And they were fully aware of the fact that if they said they needed to break the bank on Social Security, I'd say right off the bat there was no way we were going to reach an agreement. As long as the proposals were reasonable, there was no reason not to reach an agreement.

But that changed after Miguel Ángel Blanco was murdered, when – as I've said already – the Basque Nationalist Party decided to pull the rug out from under the non-violence pact. That was a serious betrayal. But I still tried to help the nationalists join in Spanish political life, taking part in dialogue and exchange.

There were a couple of other points in those conversations that made any pact impossible from the beginning. We demanded that the Basque Nationalist Party come out emphatically and unconditionally against terrorism, leaving no room for ambiguity. But, as we later saw, they were looking for something else: alibis and excuses for possible political negotiations.

Ardanza said we had to turn back the clocks and start negotiating from scratch. But, of course, the terrorist clock was still running and the Basque Statute had already been negotiated, promulgated and accepted. So what exactly was going to be turned back? Were we supposed to negotiate a new Statute, and do so under threat of terror? Reopen negotiations that accept terrorism as viable action?

That was totally unthinkable. I would never, ever do anything like that. And that's why, when they came out with the Ibarretxe Plan in 2003, it became clear that this was just a new way of dressing up old plans first laid out in the Estrella Pact. What made it even worse was that they wanted to sit down at the table and reach an agreement with ETA.

A Model for Integration

There is such a thing as nationalism without terrorism and, as we've seen over these years, nationalism can make a positive contribution to the country as a whole. However, it's a limited contribution. At one extreme you've got terrorism and at the other the boundaries laid out by nationalism itself, boundaries exemplified, for instance, by Convergència i Unió's refusal to participate in national government.

I don't think nationalism is part of our future. I think that wherever it takes hold, it blocks the road to progress. Nationalism needs an enemy to focus on, and that leads to defensive positions that take away from any integration potential and lead to confrontation and internal disintegration.

Some Spanish regional nationalism confronts the very idea of Spain, and some Spanish nationalists opposed the idea of Europe. Anti-Americanism is part of a certain conception of Europe that isn't far off nationalism. All of these things are unadvisable because they limit opportunities, create unnecessary barriers and instill fear and insecurity by trying to convince people that there is some foreign enemy out there, when there really isn't.

It's even worse in a country like Spain, where language and cultural diversity are not only respected but recognized and supported by the Constitution, the Statues, the national government, local governments and every political and administrative body in the country. Movements for recognition are understandable in countries where certain groups are treated unfairly or even banned. But that's not the case here, where absolute freedom is guaranteed and the state actively defends it.

Our position, our obligation, is to ensure that the rules of the democratic game are followed. Democracy is safeguarded by certain things. That was proved, for example, when Herri Batasuna was banned. And the law provides the state the instruments it needs to make opportune decisions, though it would be fabulous if none of those decisions ever had to be made.

A broad, solid consensus amongst national parties is vital on this point. That's why the Socialists' current actions are particularly worrisome. The stronger and more solid the national party agreements, the less chance there is of this type of movement being started.

Then again, we also have to fill in the cracks that might crop up along the way in given circumstances. If anyone decides to call a referendum without following the rules - which is totally illegal - then we'd have to decide whether that's considered a crime and how to classify that crime - something that until now has been inconceivable - would have to be set out. Democracy spells out general rules that then have to be defined specifically by political, legal or judicial actions. That's what we have to outline over time, as the need arises;

it's not something that happens all at once. The instruments used to defend democracy and legality at the state's disposal need to be used if the circumstances so require.

The New Spaniards

According to December 2003 figures, the population of Spain is now 42,717,064. We've never had so many people. This includes 1,647, 011 legal immigrants. Spain has gone from being a country of emigrants to one of immigrants. We used to have all the problems characteristic of poorer countries; now we face the problems of developed ones. The difference is that the problems faced by poorer countries are harder to solve. Emigration was the result of poverty, and that's hard to reverse. The problems that developed countries confront can be managed and resolved. Immigration is an indication of how much Spain and the problems it faces have changed.

This huge change occurred in a very short period of time, the exact same time that it took for the Spanish economy to begin to grow. People now arrive in search of work and they have to assimilate, they have rights, they have health and educational needs, and they're in need of services. Right now there are almost a million immigrants contributing to Social Security.

Immigration presents challenges that, in terms of integration and assimilation, are a little easier for us in Spain, because a large number of our immigrants come from Latin America so we share a history, culture and language. We've also got immigrants from the rest of Europe who buy property and come here to retire, because of the climate, the services, and – let's be honest – because Spain is a great place to live.

So immigration offers us great opportunities, but also presents us with challenges that we have to face up to.

Spain's history is a universal one. Spanish culture has spread through the Atlantic, the Americas and even into the Pacific like few other countries. I've already discussed the Spanish language's wide-ranging and varied cultures, and I've referred to the diversity of Spain's culture as well. We've exported our culture and yet we've also managed to preserve it at home. So we have no reason to fear globalization or to fear the arrival of people in search of job opportunities, who want to contribute to the common good with their efforts.

I know we're a relatively open country, capable of welcoming people of different backgrounds and treating them equally. Spaniards are a tolerant bunch, and they're not afraid of people whose customs are different from their own.

Spain's ability to assimilate immigrants has been very impressive, especially considering how fast the phenomenon of immigration developed here. Obviously we've seen new problems that we need to confront. So it's logical that we've had to reform our legislation in light of changing circumstances. We've had to avoid any measures that could hamper the immigrants' ability to integrate into Spanish society.

On the other hand, our newfound prosperity also brought on different problems: illegal immigration, the mafia that organizes and takes advantage of it, and international organized crime. A prosperous country like Spain is not only attractive to immigrants in search of new opportunities. It's also attractive to international crime and drug trafficking networks. Spain is a border country in the European Union, which means we have to exert a considerable effort to tackle the flow of illegal immigration.

We need to cooperate with the countries these immigrants are coming from, but regardless of how much we help them, how generous we are, it will be a long time before they are prosperous enough to stem the flow of people trying to leave. Meanwhile, we'll have to find a way to maintain order within the flow of immigration and insist on the importance of legal immigration and work permits. We can't just embark on a permanent naturalization process for our immigrant population. We have to foresee their problems and channel them as best we can.

At any rate, immigration is extraordinarily important in terms of our national prosperity, the rate at which it's growing – which indicates its enormous economic and social potential – and also in terms of the immigrants themselves. Many of them, people who are willing to work, to save, and to make their homes in Spain, will settle here, educate their children as Spaniards and become Spaniards themselves. They are Spaniards out of choice. That's a historic change.

Spain as Nation

Since the signing of the Constitution in 1978, Spain as a nation has been extraordinarily open and generous. Spain has been open to every opportunity, to all kinds of input. We've taken on board and will continue to take on board all of the proposed contributions, all the different paths we can explore. The future is bright for anyone with a project, a dream.

All we demand in exchange is loyalty. We've tried every possible means of explaining this, making it clear that people have to be loyal to the nation that has allowed them to do whatever they like, realize their dreams, speak the language they want, practice any of the cultural traditions that make up Spanish culture. I'm sure the immense majority of Spaniards agree with that demand.

We'll keep on allowing all those things, because that's our duty and because we want to. But no one should take that as a sign of weakness. There is no weakness in our system now, nor is there any room for weakness in the future.

I've always been convinced that, in the long run, the country can overcome this loyalty problem. The first thing we have to do is admit that it exists. For a long time there have been national political forces that feel guilty about nationalism. They feel guilty about the left, too, so there's a double complex there.

I've never had any complex about either one of those things. I respect all positions, but why should I have a complex if I don't share those positions? I've been willing to make as many pacts as necessary.

But when the time comes, we've got to be perfectly clear: the forest, as I said before, is not to be razed, partitioned up, or burned down. The forest is diverse and we have to maintain its diversity, as we have for the past twenty-five years.

Spain's pluralistic roots stem from the Constitution. And that's what I defend: the Constitution, and what's at its core, which is the national unity that makes plurality, diversity, cooperation and tolerance possible.

Spain is once again on the road to becoming a great nation. For a long time it was a first-rate nation and it should never have stopped being one. Spain is set to become a country as great and as important as we want it to be.

Obviously, Spain has a long history, and we don't have to like all of it. But that doesn't make us any less Spanish or any less obliged to continue our own historic path. And that means not going back and making the same mistakes we once made. We all know what they cost our parents and ourselves. We've been very successful over the past twenty-five years. We've worked and sacrificed to make that success possible. Now we face an extraordinary opportunity. We can't let that go to waste. I've tried to defend our historic continuity and constitutionality. Those are the conditions for prosperity and freedom.

After the March 11th Attack

On March 11, 2004, I received word of the Madrid attacks at 7:30am, just after the bombs went off in the Atocha, El Pozo and Santa Eugenia train stations. I realized the gravity of the situation immediately. And, like everyone else, I became progressively more aware of the true dimensions of the tragedy as the news updates came in, jumbled and catastrophic.

My first concern, and the government's first concern, was for the victims. Saving lives, tending to the wounded, and helping the families and friends of those affected find their loved ones are the most important things at a time like this. It is the number one priority. Anyone who suffers a terrorist attack must know from the first second that they can count on the government and all the state institutions to support them, no matter what.

At the same time, the government has a duty to restore order and normality as quickly as possible. A terrorist attack is always a defeat, but showing that terrorism cannot sow panic and disorder is crucial; it's a start, a way to regain ground. We had to make it clear that we refused to be afraid and that Spanish society refused to give in to any attack.

I feel an incredible debt of gratitude to all those who made such an effort that morning, helping the victims and lending a hand with the relief operation on the scene. The Community of Madrid, the city council, the national train network (RENFE), firemen and security forces, doctors and health workers, IFEMA (Madrid's trade fair) workers, cleaners, taxi drivers...everyone who volunteered to help ease the suffering and restore order has my greatest respect and deepest admiration and appreciation. The Royal Family, as always, set an example for us all.

I am proud to live in a city and be a citizen of a country that reacted as the people of Madrid - and Spain - did in those tragic moments. It set an example for us all, and it was a great consolation. Terrorists had taken nearly two hundred lives, injured fifteen hundred people, and deeply and permanently scarred friends and loved ones. But in their response, the Spanish public showed that, regardless of their anguish, they refused to be terrified by those who sought to destroy them.

As the government lent its attention to the victims and to restoring as much order and normality as possible given the circumstances, the investigation into what had happened was launched. I initially thought, as did all the government, that ETA had carried out the attacks. We weren't the only ones in Spain or abroad to reach those conclusions. There was not a single state representative or media source advancing any other hypothesis at that time. It fit, given the terrorist actions that security forces had thwarted in the preceding months, such as on Christmas Eve 2003 and on February 2004, when a truck loaded with 500 kilos of dynamite was intercepted in Cuenca. And like all of ETA's recent attempts, this one was not set for any random town in Spain; it was aimed at Madrid.

After the Cuenca incident, some Socialists went so far as to doubt the government's counter-terrorist operations, suggesting that the capture of the 500-kilo truckload of dynamite (the March 11 attacks used 100 kilos) was staged. And there's something else to bear in mind: we were about to finish election campaigns and the elections were four days away when all this occurred. Surveys had shown the Popular Party winning, and although of course these speculations are just that – speculations – more than once over the course of that tragic morning I thought about how the attacks might be read after the elections were over, the meaning that might be attached to their possible influence at the polls.

Only time will tell whether the attacks played a role in the outcome or not. But we've learned a lesson: terrorist violence cannot be used for party political aims. It's unethical, for one, and open, democratic societies like ours won't put up with it. The only thing we'll ever allow terrorism to do is reaffirm the principles that uphold peace and freedom.

The belief that ETA had carried out the attack, unanimously supported at first, was corroborated by certain indications that the immediate investigation uncovered. During the eight years I've been in office, the government's counter-terrorist policy has always rested on two indisputable principles: respect for the law, and respect for truth. I've never hidden the aims of our counter-terrorist operations or the steps taken in order to perform them from anyone. Out of respect for the Spanish public, for the basic rules of our policy and for democracy we stuck to those principles as soon as we found indications that an Islamic fundamentalist group might have been responsible for the Madrid attacks.

The Minister of the Interior, acting on my orders and his own sense of duty, made new information available to the public and updated it whenever possible, every time that new data was uncovered. I have nothing but pride and admiration for the security forces and the National Center for Intelligence, who covered a tremendous amount of ground in a very short time and kept on with their discoveries and analyses, keeping several lines of investigation open. For reasons that should be obvious to everyone, the government cannot advance any hypotheses or speculations based on rumor. Our duty is to make the facts, and actions resulting from the facts, known to the public; that's what we did whenever it was necessary and as quickly as possible.

I respect all those who were honestly worried about the possibility that the government, including myself, was hiding information. What's more, I think this level of mistrust is a sign of a mature democracy, one that's more aware of its own strength than some people realize. I assure those citizens that just as I have always told the truth about the fight against terrorism, the government has also been open about the information it was receiving during the course of the investigation.

The declassification of the National Center for Intelligence documents on the investigation was an attempt to address this – legitimate – concern. It wasn't a simple attempt at exoneration. Without compromising the integrity of the investigation, those documents reinforce what I've already remarked on: the professionalism and accomplishment of those in charge of our security.

I've always said, and I've reiterated over the course of this book, that terrorism is never justified; it diminishes the legitimacy of the cause it alleges to support. I believe we should fight all terrorists the same way: with no concessions, and flatly refusing to be blackmailed. The way I see it, both ETA and Islamic fundamentalist terrorism warrant the same treatment, the same rejection. However, I must admit that until March 11th, Spanish public opinion was perhaps not sufficiently aware of the scope of the Islamic terrorist threat. Or at least not as aware of it as they were of the threat posed by ETA. If that's the case, there's no doubt that the government has to assume responsibility. Perhaps the very success of our fight against ETA in the past few years led us to drop our guard with respect to the fundamentalist threat. And maybe we've caused some confusion with regard to our role in the fight against terror, as if we'd agreed to take part in it in exchange for help fighting the battles we've got here on our own home ground.

It was never my aim to confuse anyone or to add to the feeling that we had no need to mobilize against the fundamentalist threat. September 11th and the investigations that have taken place since then clearly demonstrate that the Islamic fundamentalist terrorist network is global, including Europe, and Spain. In some instances we've detected its movements in time. Unfortunately, on March 11th, we didn't. Spaniards, Europeans, and particularly politicians and leaders should ask ourselves how these networks have managed to go undetected by security forces and what it is that our societies offer the terrorists who want to destroy them. Here, too, we've learned a lesson. At too high a price, and one that will grieve us forever. But we've learned something we should have known long ago: that in a world as open as ours, no border guarantees immunity from attack.

On March 12th, barely a day and a half after the attacks, more than 11 million people took to the streets to protest, show their pain, pay their respects to the victims, demonstrate their loyalty to the Constitution and to democracy, and express their condemnation of terrorism. It was the biggest anti-terrorist demonstration we had ever seen in Spain, or in Europe. Since Miguel Ángel Blanco's assassination in July 1998 there had never been anything like it. And never had so many people felt the need to condemn terrorism so resoundingly, so unwaveringly. In July 1998 an entire nation came together, united in pain, to prove that terrorism could be defeated. On March 12th they did it again.

Just as we must learn many lessons from the tragedy itself, so must we learn from the expressions of indignation, rejection and affirmation. The same generous, compassionate Spain that acted on March 11th expressed its views on the 12th. There was no doubt as to what our country's stance on terror is. And we'll have to keep that up, and use it to our advantage. After the fog of political confrontation clears, we'll still have that sweeping rejection that comes out of respect for the victims and the pain felt by the friends and family they left behind. The March 12th demonstration should serve as an inspiration and a wake-up call to us all. Because pretending it never happened is an act of betrayal and disloyalty.

The government that won the March 14th elections has a special responsibility in that sense. They have to translate what the people expressed that afternoon into actions. And they have a special responsibility to the truth. The truth was invoked ceaselessly on the days between March 11th and the March 14th elections. My government has proved it told the truth: the truth about the details that were emerging, the truth about the scope of the investigation, and the truth about the hypotheses being formulated as we learned new information.

There were some people - in particular the Socialist candidate's campaign advisor, now acting as head of the PSOE parliamentary group - who told the media on the night of March 13th that the government was lying. Now that these grave accusations have been proven false, these people - who knowingly violated the electoral law that banned them from making any political statements on the day of reflection - have the duty to prove that their accusations were not intentionally predisposed to express something they knew not to be true. And if they can't prove it and don't act accordingly, then the public will know what to expect from them. The people, aware of the possibility of being manipulated or having information held from them, deserve nothing less.

I have nothing but confidence in my country's democracy. We are a mature, responsible society. And the people demand from their government what any democracy should: respect for public opinion, respect for the law, and respect for truth and transparency. I have no doubt about the legitimacy of the government that won the March 14th elections. Time will put things in their place and, just as we'll all find out the truth about what happened between March 12th and March 14th, we'll also find out who then acted accordingly.

Right now, I can say two things. One, I repeat that my government abided by the information it received. And two, what happened on the March 13th day of reflection deserves utter condemnation by any democratic citizen respecting the law. The illegal demonstrations, the shouting outside the Popular Party headquarters, the insults directed at the government, and the defamation campaign were attempts to tarnish the civic spirit of the demonstrations held the day before. They didn't achieve their aim then, and they never will.

It wasn't the first time my party members and activists have been harassed by others who claim we lack the authority not just to govern but to exist. We saw that in the March 12th demonstrations in

Barcelona when two Popular Party representatives were prevented from expressing their condolences to the victims. This kind of act contradicts the spirit of tolerance that has characterized Catalonian public life up until now. We saw it in the campaign against the Popular Party during the Iraq War, when they not only expressed legitimate dissent at the government's decisions but also tried to deny the government's legitimacy. The night of March 13th Mariano Rajoy, the Popular Party presidential candidate, denounced the harassment the party was suffering at their own headquarters in Madrid and the flagrant violation of electoral law by those who perpetrated and instigated it.

Those who had the moral obligation to echo this condemnation didn't do it. Rather than attempt to quell public opinion, already alarmed at the gravity of what was occurring, they acted as spokespeople for those who were hurling insults on the streets and in the media. I trust that this will never happen again. It's behavior unworthy of the Spanish public, unworthy of twenty-five years of democracy, of the dialogue and tolerance that have prevailed over our nation's recent history. What happened over the course of those few days shows that a lot of people who throw around serious words like dialogue and tolerance are not necessarily willing to put them into practice when the tables are turned. It's not easy, of course. But the March 11th attacks were a cry for us all to come together out of respect for the recent victims, so the divisiveness shown by some is even more undignified.

Some people tried to bring the old Spain of civil confrontation back to life on March 13th. They didn't manage, of course, nor will they. The Spain I live in, the 9.5 million voters who backed the Popular Party on March 14th, won't let us go back to that. And I'm sure that even the majority of those who didn't vote for us agree. The new government will be making a serious mistake if they think that the March 13th demonstrations seen on some streets and in the media are any way to establish democratic national policy.

Over the last few years, Spain has taken on an increasingly important international role, with all of the attendant commitments. We joined the European Union, which was the natural geographical and political space in which to develop; we joined the Atlantic Alliance, thereby undertaking the responsibility to defend Western cultural values; and we've taken part in several military and peace-keeping missions. On certain occasions, such as in Afghanistan in 2002, this has been under United Nations mandate. On others, such as the 1992-1993 Bosnia mission, there has been no express UN mandate but we acted under the command of the Socialist government. In all cases there was a broad international consensus with regard to the threats posed and the need to respond.

When US and UK troops invaded Iraq and toppled the Iraqi regime in March 2003, there was a general conviction that the regime posed a threat both to its neighbors and to the West. The international community knew, as did we, that the regime had not allowed United Nations weapons inspectors to carry out their tasks, and that they would not facilitate inspections in the future. We don't know what happened to the weapons of mass destruction that the Bagdad regime had. But we do know that they had them: they proved it in the war they declared on Iran and they used them to massacre their own people, especially many thousands of Kurds and Shiites. We knew then, as we know now – and anyone who denies this falls short of the truth – that Saddam Hussein never proved he had discontinued plans to manufacture them. That is what the UN resolutions that supported the Coalition of the Willing were based on.

Spain didn't take part in the war, though we did support the allies combating the threat the Iraqi regime posed. We did, however, commit 1,300 soldiers to help in the peace-keeping effort and to help build a tolerant, civilized regime that will respect human rights in Iraq.

One of the components of the new international order that came out of the fall of the Berlin Wall and the September 11th attacks is that we have new responsibilities and must take on new commitments. I said that in an earlier chapter and I'll say it again now. It's not like the

Cold War, when you had regular armies that respected rules, that respected civilian populations and believed borders were inviolable and acted accordingly. The enemies we now face don't respect borders, and civilians are no longer safe. The September 11th attacks and the attacks in Iraq after the capture of Saddam Hussein – many of which are directed against civilians and some particularly violent attacks have even been directed against the UN – along with attacks in Istanbul, Bali, Casablanca and Madrid all make that perfectly clear. Borders are no longer sacred.

Responding to that threat requires a strong, unwavering commitment, and a refusal to give in to corruption. I'll come back to this. It also means that prosperous, developed democracies have to commit to help set up living conditions in those countries that will enable them to eradicate fanaticism and senseless violence. Free countries – wealthy countries – have to help the regimes in countries where terrorist movements have arisen – many of them Islamic countries - take steps towards ensuring that their people can live free, dignified, decent lives. It's not an impossible feat; there are non-Western democracies. But it's a long, hard, thankless road.

Some people in Spain have the audacity to claim that our soldiers were part of an occupation, that they were subjugating Iraq and obstructing the sovereignty of a free country. That's just not true. Iraq was not a free country under Saddam Hussein. And it's still not free today, but that's because it's being wracked by brutal terrorism, terrorism that reached our shores on March 11th as it reached three thousand people in New York and Washington on September 11th, long before the allies went into Iraq.

Our troops were in Iraq to help restore order and to save lives, just as the security forces did for the citizens of Madrid on March 11th. They were in Iraq to repair and build infrastructure, and to support the authority that reached a consensus on a Constitution for all Iraqis. Iraq needs our help. They've told us this on numerous occasions.

Spain has been, and should continue to be, one of the most active countries in the democratic fight against terrorism. We shouldn't leave the defense of freedoms we enjoy solely to the US or Great Britain, thereby washing our hands of the commitment to our defense. We can't become a country that depends wholly on decisions made in Washington and London for our own national and international security. We have to play a part in those decisions; they affect us more each day.

Before March 11th we were already painfully aware of terrorist violence. Now we feel it even more. Terrorism will keep striking out wherever it can. The victims of terror are international, whether in New York, Bali, Mombassa, Casablanca, Istanbul, Karbala or Madrid, where people from many different countries died. We had victims from Brazil, Bulgaria, Colombia, Chile, Cuba, Ecuador, Philippines, France, Guinea-Bissau, Honduras, Morocco, Peru, Poland, the Dominican Republic, Romania and the Ukraine. On March 12th the government granted them Spanish citizenship to honor their memories.

No one is safe from terrorism. This year, one German and one Dutch engineer were murdered in Iraq for committing the crime of laying pipes to carry drinking water. Terrorists threatened France after the French Parliament put restrictions on wearing religious symbols at school. Islamic terrorism has already proven it can strike in Europe, and if we show signs of weakness now, it will intensify.

This is a fight between freedom, democracy and civilization on one side, and terror, fanaticism and totalitarianism on the other. On September 11th we were all American. On March 11th, the whole world was Spanish, and the Spanish public was all from Madrid. The world saw us face our adversity with strength, serenity and courage. We have to keep it up. We can't lose the spirit. We have to give it our all in order to win this fight.

Throughout my political career, and especially during my eight years as Prime Minister, I've always said that terrorism is not a local phenomenon, it's not something you only find in one region or one country; you can't fight it with one-off measures. Terrorism is global and knows no bounds. If we think it's someone else's problem, someone else's responsibility, then we only make it stronger.

The investigation into who committed the March 11th attacks in Madrid is very important, because we need to know who was behind them. But terrorism always carries the same threat. All terrorist attacks show the same hatred of freedom, democracy and human dignity. There's no difference between people who resort to terror in an attempt to achieve certain aims; their strength feeds on the wounds opened by an attack, regardless of who carries it out.

Before September 11th all Spanish governments, including those prior to the Popular Party administration, made an effort to show the civilized world that terrorism wasn't an isolated phenomenon and that the responsibility of fighting it should not fall solely to the victims. After the Twin Towers fell, we started to see a new attitude towards terrorism, one that responded to the position Spanish leaders had always held in international forums.

ETA and Al Qaeda: the differences are not irrelevant, but the response should be the same: strength, political unity and international cooperation. The Madrid commuter trains were filled with democratic citizens that March 11th morning. It was an attack on us all, on everything we believe in, on everything we've built.

That's why we shouldn't send mixed messages, messages that will lead people to believe we've made concessions to people who are asking us to kneel and beg forgiveness for living in democracy, for enjoying freedom, for having created prosperous societies. Now is not the time to pull the troops out of Iraq. Especially when the terrorists have just told us, with their message of death and destruction, that we should give up.

We've refused to give up in the face of ETA and we know what would have happened if we had. Pulling the troops out of Iraq will be interpreted the same way: as a sign of weakness. That's probably not what's intended, but let's not fool ourselves. If the troops are withdrawn, the terrorists will be convinced that they managed to influence Spain's international position on terrorism. They'll believe they changed the make-up of the international coalition fighting against them. A move like this could carry incredibly grave consequences. Pulling out of Iraq in these circumstances will set a dangerous precedent. The terrorists will think they've managed to impose their conditions on us. They'll think they've won.

Spain's new position on the international front is a direct result of our international policy. But our increasing sphere of influence shouldn't be seen as an end in and of itself. It's a means to better serve national interests and to attend to our citizens and their needs. The values and principles that have guided our foreign policy stem from the government's axes of domestic policy: defending freedom and fighting terrorism; promoting our languages and cultures, whose plurality are guaranteed by the Constitution; opening up our economy via liberalization measures; helping defend human dignity.

In the eight years I've had the honor to serve my country as Prime Minister, we've come a long way. We've made great progress on the road we started down in 1996. I think it's fair to say – and the statistics prove this – that citizens today are better off and have more opportunities, more freedom.

These advances would not have been possible if we hadn't built a solid base for our prosperity. The Spanish public will have to decide if they want to keep building on that or if they want to dismantle it, brick by brick, reform by reform. Our future is not set in stone. The decisions that we – each and every one of us – make now will decide whether we continue to advance our economic and institutional stability. Or move backwards.

We often think that, when things are going well, they'll keep going well, that progress doesn't turn back on itself, that the prosperity we see today won't just disappear tomorrow. But history – even the history of our country – is full of examples to the contrary.

Spain today, in 2004, is on the verge of attaining the quality of life and prestige of the world's very greatest nations. This historic opportunity could be wasted if we don't maintain proven economic policies based on austerity, limits on state expenditure, the promotion of initiative and individual freedom and respect for the law and the truth.

It will also be endangered if we get caught up in discussions on the organization of our state, discussions that – I'm convinced – concern the general public even less than they do the handful of politicians who are more interested in power than they are in society. Spain's progress over the last twenty-five years has been based on the stability provided by the 1978 constitutional framework.

Today, the blueprint for a state that came out of the Constitution is a reality. We've all helped build a nation that's consistent with our country's make-up: a decentralized administration that can solve problems and channel our rich, cultural and linguistic plurality.

Now we can choose one of two paths. We can strengthen and reinforce this framework so our economy continues to take off and we increase prosperity and well-being for all. Or we can cast doubt on it, reopen the constitutional debate and resurrect the whole territorial question. To do this is to risk our future. It will have consequences for Spain's international position, because it will create a climate of distrust - especially economically – which will jeopardize our growth, as well as endangering foreign investment. It will weaken us abroad, in the eyes of our allies and in the eyes of those who attacked us during the March 11th electoral campaign. There will also be national consequences, because instead of concentrating on what common sense and our common experience dictate, which is to keep striving for even greater prosperity and unity, we'll find ourselves bogged down in futile arguments that belong in the past, things that will pull us back in every area, including history.

People know where I'll be; they know where the Popular Party will be. My whole life, I've strived to keep my promises. We promised we'd become one of Europe's leading nations and we're now on the cusp of that. We promised to increase our citizen's prosperity and we've done that. We promised to finalize the model for an open, pluralistic state. We've done that, too. I personally promised that I'd step down after eight years as Prime Minister. And I have.

I know not everyone agrees with my personal convictions and

my politics. We didn't spend the last eight years in search of unanimity or a continuous round of applause. But our policies were always guided by a profound respect for commitment, personal dignity and the truth. It's not easy, but I've always made an effort to tell the truth. Throughout my early political career, then when I was Prime Minister, and most recently as soon as I found out what had happened in Madrid, when sickening tragedy overcame us all.

Having told the truth in such tough times, there's no reason to conceal it now, when fewer responsibilities weigh upon me, and the Popular Party - through the Spanish public's legitimate decision - has gone back to being an opposition party. Now more than ever, I need to stand up and tell the truth. And I promise to do just that: to state what I believe to be true, whenever I feel it necessary. Whoever doubts that is making a mistake. Because that's one way we'll offer compatriots a serious, trustworthy alternative to the government. As serious and trustworthy as our last eight years in power have been.

GLOSSARY

AP   Alianza Popular   Popular Alliance
Conservative party founded in 1976 by Manuel Fraga. In 1989 it became the PP, which shifted significantly towards the center.

CiU   Convergència i Unió   Convergence and Union
Catalonian coalition party led by Jordi Pujol, President of the *Generalitat* (Catalonian autonomous government) from 1980 to 2003

HB   Herri Batasuna   Herri Batasuna
The political wing of ETA, HB was declared illegal in 1997.

PNV   Partido Nacional Vasco   Basque Nationalist Party

PP   Partido Popular   Popular Party
Aznar's party, founded in 1989, whose leadership was taken over by Mariano Rajoy when Aznar stepped down in 2004.

PSOE   Partido Socialista Obrero Español   Socialist Party
Currently led by José Luis Rodríguez Zapatero, Prime Minister of Spain. Previously led by Felipe González, Prime Minister from 1982 to 1996.

UCD   Unión de Centro Democrático   Democratic Center Union
Party formed by Adolfo Suárez in 1977 and dissolved in 1983. Central to Spain's transition to democracy after nearly 40 years of dictatorship under Francisco Franco. A moderate alternative to the left, opposed to Francoist reform.